Becoming A Digital Marketer

gaining the hard & soft skills
for a tech-driven marketing career

GIL & ANYA GILDNER

Becoming A Digital Marketer:
Gaining the Hard & Soft Skills For A
Tech-Driven Marketing Career

Copyright © 2019 by Gil & Anya Gildner
www.discosloth.com

ISBN 978-1-7337948-7-9

Published by Baltika Press
www.baltikapress.com

Cover image by Ronaldo Arthur Vidal.

Printed in the United States of America.

ACKNOWLEDGEMENTS

Thank you to our editor, Anna Packer, her tireless eye for detail, and for encouraging us to avoid using the word "nice" so much. Thanks to Riel Manriquez for hiring us into the same company, to Jack Shock and Jim Miller for instilling a nice passion for communication into so many young folks, to all the nice people who told us not to quit our jobs, to our nice clients, and especially thanks to the many nice cups of coffee it took to write this book.

CONTENTS

WHAT IS MARKETING?

"If you've invented something new but you haven't invented an effective way to sell it, you have a bad business—no matter how good the product." - Peter Thiel [1]

The American Marketing Association says that "marketing is the activity, set of institutions, and processes for creating, communicating, delivering, and exchanging offerings that have value for customers, clients, partners, and society at large."

I think that's a little verbose, uses too much jargon, and doesn't really capture the spirit of marketing. You'd think such a prominent organization would be able to, well, market themselves a little better?

The Merriam-Webster dictionary, on the other hand, says marketing is "the action or business of promoting and selling products or services, including market research and advertising."

This is much closer to the spirit of the thing.

The word *marketing* comes, in a roundabout way, from the Latin word *mercari*, which meant "buy." This word evolved into the word *mercatus*, which blended with the word *merchant*, and eventually became the verb *market*.

But *to market* is totally different than simply *to sell*. That's why we have two different words. Selling something is the act of trading one thing for another (taking money in exchange for a loaf of bread, for example). Marketing, however, is the art of letting people know about that tasty loaf of bread. It's the practice of getting that bread in front of people and convincing them to buy it.

In reality, I think you can boil marketing down to four simple words: *selling things through stories.*

That story - the tale through which you sell something - can take a lot of forms. It can be descriptive, covering all the essential facts about the bread, like what grain it's made from, how many calories it contains, or how healthy it is. It can be emotional - where the recipe came from, how it smells, or the culture from which it originates. Or, it can be entirely brand-focused - *who* made the bread?

There is nothing new under the sun.

Digital marketing is just the latest iteration of a vendor hawking his wares in an ancient market. Digital marketing just happens to take place on the internet, rather than a dusty, crowded street in ancient Egypt.

Because the internet is so vast (3.2 billion users at last count), it's also much more complicated than the strictly physical marketplaces of old. Thousands of miles, languages, laws, cultures, and industries are between us and our audience now, and it's a lot harder to gain crucial initial traction. But this isn't necessarily a downside: it means there are also thousands more possibilities and opportunities as well.

The majority of websites on the internet are in English - around 55%, as of 2018. But if you speak only English, imagine that as big as the internet is, you're only seeing *half* of it. The second most common language in use on websites is Russian, followed by German, Japanese, Spanish, and French.[2]

The internet is huge, and it's just growing more every day. While internet adoption rates in the developed world have pretty much capped, the developing world is rapidly expanding, and there are still billions more people to go before we reach the stage of everyone utilizing the internet. There is still a lot of time to be a part of the internet's growth.

I never liked business books. Business books try to give you a formula for success, which, if applied in the real world, will only lead to mediocrity at best. If there was a formula for outsized success, everyone would have followed it, and everyone would have seen unicorn-level rates of success, fame, and riches. No such thing!

This is not a business book. It's just a bunch of stories sandwiched between technical, descriptive sections. There is no formula for success, only a picture of what has worked in the past, and your job as a reader is to take the various bits of information and combine them into a strategy that works for you.

Everyone is different, and things change fast. By the time you're reading this book, there are already a hundred new digital marketing strategies and a dozen new channels to implement ad campaigns on. The hard skills rapidly become outdated.

If you can learn one single thing from this book, it's that in order to be a successful digital marketer, you've got to keep on the forefront of things, and then keep on going. As soon as you learn one thing, it's already outdated. As soon as you hear about another thing, it's already clogged with users. But as long as you keep yourself on the cusp of the industry, try new things, and learn how to teach yourself new technologies and strategies, you'll be just fine.

We'll start by going over the wide range of digital marketing channels in use today, beginning with organic search (using search engine optimization to get websites ranking well on search engines like Google or Bing), and from there we'll venture into paid search (implementing and managing paid ad campaigns on those same search engines). These two channels in and of themselves are perhaps the largest slices of the digital marketing pie, so we'll spend a lot of time going into depth on search marketing.

After that, we'll look at social media: using organic social strategies, advertising on social platforms, and exploring influencer marketing.

Then we'll look at content marketing, which overlaps with most of the other channels but still deserves a section for itself. This includes video creation and distribution, writing for the web, and audio marketing with content, like podcasts.

We can't ignore email marketing: even if it seems like an old-fashioned way of marketing, it's still one of the most profitable and ignored channels by the modern marketer.

And finally, we'll go over traditional marketing channels, because if you work in the marketing industry long enough you'll need to align your marketing efforts with all sorts of other channels.

After we look at all of these channels, we'll go on to some hard and soft skills required to be successful in marketing.

Hard skills are actually the least of your worries: as long as you are fairly tech-savvy and good with computers, you'll be fine. We'll cover web development skills, multimedia editing, reporting and analytics, and even a few tricky marketing fads that are best ignored.

Soft skills are hard to learn, but invaluable. These include writing persuasive copy, time management, writing solid business emails, general marketing theory, project management and process, and even a little bit of sales.

After the skills part, we'll go into the business side of things. Whether you want to work for a marketing agency, or work for an in-house marketing department, or even start freelancing as a marketer, we'll cover all of these and also offer insight from others who have walked the same steps, not long before you.

Next, we'll include a little section on starting your own marketing business. Even if you don't plan on doing this yourself, it's worth learning about since more marketers are now quitting their traditional jobs and starting their own companies. It gives you the ability to work entirely remotely and have the potential to make more money than traditional employment roles, so at the minimum, there's a chance you will work with a lot of these people throughout your career. We'll cover legal and financial structure, how to get clients, how to brand yourself, how to charge, and some practicalities like accounting and invoicing.

Finally, we'll close with some thoughts about the future of work. Because going to an office from nine to five is so…1990s.

You'll find that this book is written from my first person perspective (I'm Gil!), but it's a joint effort. And, if we're being honest, most of the real information in the book comes from Anya's brain. I'm just the opinionated purveyor.

OUR STORY, FROM CRADLE TO COMPANY

Gil's story begins in front of a computer.

A fifty-pound grey Dell tower, to be exact, with a loud fan, a clicking floppy drive, and a cheap plastic mouse with a tracking ball clogged with hair. Sometime around 2004, I found an old copy of Macromedia Dreamweaver, and like any socially normal fourteen-year-old, I installed it, started dissecting websites and building my own. Growing up in the early 2000s meant that I'd missed the true wild-west heyday of the internet, but I was on the tail end of it. Webmastering wasn't really a career anymore, but even simple tech savviness went a long way in rural Arkansas. I built websites for contractors, churches, schools, and musicians.

During college, I flittered aimlessly between programs. I finally found the promised land of communication: the art of telling stories and getting paid to do so. I took a summer off to go to film school in Los Angeles, where I spent a semester learning from a mean, old, mustached French animation professor in a hot, sweaty building in Hollywood. I came back with a renewed, if somewhat naive, passion for filmmaking.

I graduated from college, straight into a job that paid even less than I'd made from my freelance work, but a job which gave me some of the most valuable connections I could have wished for. But I was a terrible employee. I jumped into the freelancing world. I spent the next five years editing videos, animating fundraising videos, shooting photos for annual reports, and hopping around the globe to shoot short films for nonprofits: schools in Kenya, factories in India, hospitals in South Africa, orphanages in Uganda, almost anywhere in the global south where NGOs operated. In late 2014, I went to Liberia during the Ebola outbreak to shoot a few small documentaries for fundraising efforts. This led to even more projects, and it finally felt like I was hitting my stride.

I was 26. I had been to 25 countries. I owned a backpack full of cameras, lenses, and computers. And I was burned out.

I decided to hang up the freelance jacket. I took a job as the creative director at a company that sold round-the-world airfare tickers. For the next year and a half, I worked in special projects and continued traveling. This was also where I met Anya, a nice girl from Moldova.

Anya's story also begins in front of a computer.

She grew up in the Republic of Moldova, a small landlocked country just to the south of Ukraine. She was encouraged by the common wisdom of those around her to pursue a career in accounting or medicine - but Anya wanted to be a hacker. She spent countless hours on the computer or huddled up in internet cafes, listening to Russian rock bands, hanging out with rocker punks, and generally being a misfit.

While she didn't end up hacking, she didn't become an accountant, either. After graduating from high school she moved to Bucharest where she got her bachelor's degree in advertising, then followed it up with a master's degree in marketing. After a stint working in data analysis for a multinational company, she began freelancing in paid advertising, setting up Google Ads campaigns, and eventually joined that same American travel company which sold airfare. Starting as the paid ads specialist, she rose to managing the marketing department, where she met me.

We worked very well together - enough that we realized we needed to branch off on our own. So we quit our jobs and decided to start a search marketing company. One cold evening, over a bottle of wine, we called it Discosloth (a name designed to evoke instant professional respect), registered a domain name, and that was the beginning of everything else.

Since that evening, it's come a long way. Although the first few months were slow, work started coming in, and our client list started snowballing. Within a few months, we were making more than we'd made at our previous jobs, and within a year, we were managing millions of dollars of annual ad spend, and we had onboarded clients from a dozen countries.

Working with clients like Volvo Trucks, AirTreks, MSF, Lutz Pumps, and hundreds of other small and medium businesses, we found our groove. We began offering corporate training seminars and speaking at conferences, writing detailed guides to introduce new marketers to upcoming techniques, and contributing to the industry.

That brings us to this book: *Becoming A Digital Marketer*.

Becoming a digital marketer is something almost anyone can do. Barriers to this career are almost non-existent: if you can read how-to guides, have access to the internet, and know your way around a browser and a spreadsheet, then with a healthy slice of ambition, you've got what it takes to become a successful marketer.

There are just a few things to know before you jump into the world of marketing: some hard skills that marketers are finding essential, and some soft skills that anyone in business will need to know in order to succeed.

This book will teach you which of these skills are important, and hopefully provide encouragement that you, too, can become a digital marketer.

PART I:
HARD SKILLS

SEARCH ENGINE OPTIMIZATION

"The only way to outdo, to outperform the competition is to offer something unique and something better than they have."
- Tim Soulo

In today's world, most companies have websites. But what good is a website if no one can find it? That's where search engine optimization comes in. In this chapter, we will cover the tactics and strategies involved in gaining highly engaged traffic from search engines like Google or Bing.

Search engine optimization (SEO) is the process, quite simply, of optimizing a website for search engines.

When a user heads to a search engine - whether that's Google, Bing, or Yandex - and types in a question and finds an answer through a link in the search results page, that's called appearing organically. You're not paying for results. It just means that the search engines consider your website authoritative enough to be ranked as a valid source of information.

Now, of course, the internet hasn't always been as smart as it is today. In the infancy of algorithms, search engines were easily tricked. Ranking a site in search results was more about knowing how to game the system than about actually creating valuable content. A classic example was the trick of coloring a big block of keyword text the same color as the site background. This made search engines think that the page contained relevant content. This trend continued until very recently, when machine learning finally improved enough to quantify the difference between valuable content and merely optimized content.

Through the entire history of search engines, people have tried to find loopholes and hack the system. Part of that is great: finding methods to increase your website's growth is always a good thing. It's the entire point of digital marketing! However, it's also been used and abused by an entire industry of less-than-classy characters, and from time to time, that's given the field of SEO a bad name.

Ultimately, I think that if your primary strategy is to game the system, it's a short-term strategy. Unless your organization has the manpower, foresight, and big data capability that Google has, you're playing a losing game of trying to stay one step ahead of the behemoth.

It's not that different from an old-school phone scammer, keeping a constant barrage of clever tricks up their sleeve that could be found out any time.

The problem these days, is that getting caught will get you slapped with a removal or penalization in a matter of hours: or just as soon as an unannounced algorithm update is released. There will never be a replacement for creating quality, valuable content that people organically link to, share, find useful, and come back to time after time. You can't churn through enough keyword generators to produce something that is actually valuable for a reader.

Often, marketers use strategies like funnel building (creating a series of landing pages that funnel users deeper into a checkout route), PBNs (private blog networks, which are website set up only to artificially inflate ranking factors), landing page generation (autogenerating hundreds or thousands of unique pages from lists of keywords) and a lot of cheap-hat inbound tactics. These strategies will work for a while to increase the SEO of your site. But they don't build trust. They don't make faithful customers. As a matter of fact, as demographics change and as the users of the internet become increasingly familiar with the concept of internet advertising, you'll find that these tactics are starting to repel potential business.

The key to creating high quality traffic (and not just fly-by visitors that were funneled onto your site from a landing page) is through becoming a subject authority on Google.[3] This is a long-term, carefully crafted process that requires research, analytics, and creation of a significant amount of well-written media. You want to become the source material for everyone else's newspaper articles, school reports, retweets, and thesis presentations. If you can pull this off, you'll have succeeded at SEO.

SEO requires patience. A lot of patience. It can take a long time to see results from organic optimization, but the upside to the process is that when done properly, it can last for a very long time. This unique benefit of SEO simply isn't available from advertising, which stops producing results pretty much as soon as you stop paying for the ads.

The thing about SEO is that it's a minefield. The industry is littered with white hat agencies (generally defined as using techniques that don't violate Google's guidelines), black hat agencies (using techniques that are definitely against Google's guidelines), and grey hat agencies (everything in between). There are a million different strategies for search optimization, and we would be remiss if we pretended to list or explain them all. However, it's definitely worth exploring a few of the main strategies that marketers use to increase the SEO of their clients.

There are a few ways to determine whether a strategy is legitimate. It needs to be transparent: not something to be embarrassed about, or to hide from clients. It needs to be consistently applicable: not something that just works temporarily, as a hack. It needs to be hands-on: not something that can be easily automated. It needs to be implemented publicly: not something using private pages or hidden sites. It needs to be easily tracked: not something that is vague or unmeasurable. And finally, it needs to be focused on quality rather than quantity.

Here are some ways to figure out if a strategy is legitimate, from each of the angles I just mentioned:

Transparency. If a strategy is proprietary and has hidden details a company won't share with you, something is shady. Quality SEO work is based upon improving value for your audience...and there isn't anything secret about this. If a strategist is reluctant to tell you about their secret sauce, or if they don't provide you with a comprehensive report detailing everything, be wary.

Consistency. If you've paid attention to news in the search marketing world, agencies make a big deal about Google algorithm updates like Panda or Penguin. In the end, there really shouldn't be any reason to be fearful of a Google update...unless you've used shady methods for ranking your site. Although we all like instant gratification, slow and steady growth and quality content always wins in the long run. If the authors of a strategy are worried about algorithm updates, question it.

Hands-on. In the world of SEO, the word "automation" means bots. And spam. Ever wondered why there's so much spam in your Wordpress comment moderation queue? That's someone out there trying to do a poor SEO job, trying to push millions of automated backlinks out into the internet with the hope that some of them stick. Automated tools (bots) means that more often or not, you actually will see a temporary increase in traffic. It's the instant dopamine rush, sort of like getting a lot of likes on your cute dog pic on Instagram. Fast forward a year, however, and you won't be as happy. Almost all of good SEO work is hard manual work. There's very little of it that can be automated.

Public. A few years back, creating private blog networks was one of the chief methods that SEO agencies used to rank sites for particular search terms. A PBN is a network of websites created & maintained privately, with the sole purpose of ranking other sites...there's no actual purpose or use for these websites. Then, in 2014, Google started to crack down on this method by penalizing websites with too many unnatural links. Almost overnight, a lot of websites that had employed shady SEOs saw their rankings drop like a rock, and it took a lot of manual link disavowing before they regained their positions. If your SEO strategist still uses private blog networks...be careful, and don't use them if you don't want your website to eventually sink in the rankings!

Trackable. You want everything you're doing to be provable through Google Analytics and other performance tracking software. Learn how to use Analytics so you can identify traffic sources, search queries, and engagement stats like time on page, bounce rate, and geolocation. Make sure the data from Analytics lines up with the growth your strategy should be creating. If you can't measure it, it's hard to know what works right.

Quality. In today's world, a good SEO strategy can be defined as making a website as useful as possible for the consumer. That includes a lot of onsite SEO optimization, and production of quality content marketing. The importance of long-form, educational, and easily shareable articles can't be emphasized enough. Ask to see examples of their work: make sure the stuff they produce is something you'd want to put on your own site. Google has recently made a large push towards what they call EAT: expertise, authority, and trustworthiness.[4] In other words, quality over quantity.

For example, we onboarded a client who was having major problems with their current SEO provider. We took over his campaign and started looking at the past tactics used by his previous agency. They had automated a linkbuilding campaign, generating over 22,000 links pointing towards his site, including many inappropriate domains and obviously spammy foreign sites. They reported only "big-picture" numbers, showing lots of clicks, but not detailing which countries this traffic came from. And they hadn't even done some very basic onboarding tasks like linking his Google Ads with Google Search Console (probably because they didn't want him seeing the actual data). They had also ignored over forty bad links (404 errors), but told him it was fine. One of the first things we did was disavow thousands of links from iffy domains. Then we fixed his 404 pages. Then, looking at his meta descriptions, we realized they had never even touched his copywriting. We went through and updated the top performing pages and most profitable products on his site. Within two months, his organic traffic had skyrocketed.

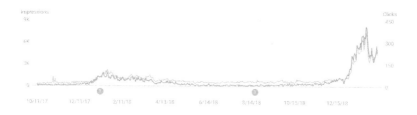

The first bump is the previous year's seasonal traffic. The second bump is after we started working on the account.

Where he was previously getting around 1000 impressions a day, he was now getting over 9000 impressions a day. And that translated into clicks: he went from an average of 50 clicks a day to over 400 clicks a day. All without building a single link.

METHODS TO EMPLOY SEO

A huge struggle with SEO is that it differs so widely according to scale. The tactics and strategies used by an enterprise-level company like IBM or 3M are vastly different than the tactics appropriate for a part-time blogger.

Because of this, much of the advice and information you find while researching best practices isn't really applicable for the beginning marketer. First, half of what you see out there are shady strategies that can get your site dinked. You want to avoid this at all costs. Much of the other half might only be applicable to large e-commerce sites, huge companies, or people with a massive existing personal brand.

But what if you don't have a brand yet?

In the first year of Discosloth, we went from registering a brand new domain and putting up a new site in a highly competitive niche, to getting tens of thousands of unique visitors and establishing ourselves as an authority with articles in the *New York Times, Washington Post, Inc Magazine*, and around 60 other sites. Our business was too precious to us to risk using "grey hat" strategies (things that work but are a little risky, like creating fake links) so none of it was done with automation, shady tactics, or paid placements.

When we started Discosloth, we started from absolute scratch. We came up with a ridiculous (yet brandable) name, registered a domain in March 2017, built a website within a week, and threw it online. We took a few months before an official hard website launch, in which we fleshed out the website, added a lot of content, and worked on the behind-the-scenes work of starting a company. When we finally decided to do a hard launch, we sent it around to friends and peers.

I wrote articles frequently, posting everywhere I possibly could: LinkedIn, Medium, and our own blog (around 40 different articles in the first year).

Starting in October of 2017, I began doing direct outreach to writers, journalists, and authority figures, using HARO (helpareporter.com) as a base. From October 2017 to June 2018, I did 64 unique HARO pitches and around 10 independent pitches to website owners and journalists.

From this, we got brand mentions in the *New York Times, Washington Post, Chicago Tribune, Inc Magazine, Arkansas Business, Democrat-Gazette, Houston Chronicle*, ABC News, CNBC, and a handful of other syndicated newspapers. We got interview snippets, full articles, and links in 14 additional websites (mostly tech blogs or marketing company blogs).

Essential to all of this was our creation of a massive piece of content, which Anya and I worked on for several months: our Beginner's Guide To PPC.[5] This was a thorough, 18,000-word resource meant to be the definitive intro for those wanting to get started in pay-per-click advertising. I sent this out to several authoritative people in the search marketing world for critique, and got some amazing feedback. Several of those people were gracious enough to promote and amplify the launch of our guide, without us even asking. The reaction was amazing, and landed us even more links, traffic, and thousands of visitors.

A year or so after the launch, our traffic had stabilized. We had extremely low numbers compared to larger, older companies in our niche, but still got thousands of visitors a month, thousands of backlinks, and hundreds of referring domains.

Now, an important caveat to note is that building natural links takes a very long time. We worked on our organic strategy for over a year to gain significant results, but as always, patience and hard work will pay off!

OFFSITE SEO: BACKLINKS

Backlinks are the doorways of the internet: links scattered across the web that direct users to other sites. You want as many of these as possible, ideally on high-quality, relevant sites. Google uses these backlinks as a ranking signal to signify that your site is authoritative and high-quality.

Building backlinks is one of the trickiest areas in SEO to execute in a white-hat manner. It's a lot of work.

Like almost any strategy in SEO, there are white-hat ways to complete your goal (and black-hat ways, too). We'll focus on the white-hat ways to gain backlinks—these are the methods that don't violate Google's user guidelines. As long as you stay on the right side of Google's guidelines, you won't be at high risk for a major traffic decline if they catch you doing something they consider unsavory. Of course, there are plenty of places to find less-than-white-hat methods, and for that I'd just encourage you to create an account over at Black Hat World. There's an entire world of tactics that live on the twilight edge of the internet, where you can buy links and create entire fake website networks - but we won't get into that here.

Google does not like when you pay for links. So, you shouldn't pay for links! Since they want you to acquire links via natural means, you need some form of valuable content on your site that people want to link to. Then, convince them to link to it.

The other way to get links is by outreach. By being an authoritative source for journalists or authors writing articles in other parts of the internet, you can get a link in return for your expertise. There are a handful of services like Help A Reporter Out, which lets you sign up to offer your endless wisdom to reporters; additionally, there are simply some hashtags to follow on Twitter (like #journorequest).

Of course, even though links from social media properties aren't considered valid per se by search engines, visibility on other channels like social media definitely sends some measure of authority to a site. Nobody is just really sure how much.

White-hat linkbuilding (the process of gaining quality links from other sites on the internet) takes a long time when it's done right, but the good news is that these legitimate links last for a long, long time. And in most cases, they're more powerful than the material any shady linkbuilding service can ever offer you (which are usually done with bots and scripts).

You can also try guest posting. This means reaching out to blogs and websites and offering to write a guest post for them. Many websites are receptive to this sort of outreach since producing content is so labor-intensive. Although this practice has been abused by many marketers, and Google doesn't always like it (some might consider it grey-hat), there are plenty of instances in which a legitimate guest poster can write an original article for a related blog, and in return, include within the article a natural link pointing back to their own site. It's just important to make sure that there's no payment involved, that the site is high quality, and that your article is a useful article. Otherwise, you can risk falling into black-hat tactics that carry more risk of a potential penalty.

ONSITE OPTIMIZATION: TECHNICAL SEO

Onsite SEO is the process of making sure your website is optimized to reap the maximum possible benefits: making it easy for search engines and users to accurately categorize and use your website. The benefits of onsite SEO (also sometimes referred to as technical SEO) are so broad, and so complex, that multiple books could be devoted to the entire subject.

The core elements of technical SEO involve analyzing a website and optimizing everything from speed, site architecture, layout, meta optimization, accessibility, internal linking, schema, canonicalization, and categorization.

Every website can benefit from excellent technical optimization, but the sites that will see the greatest benefits are huge sites with thousands of pages and an existing search presence:

especially multinational or e-commerce sites with massive numbers of products.

Google's crawlers have limited resources devoted to them, and technical SEO ensures that they are able to discover every page on the site and keep them freshly indexed. Technical optimization also increases speed and site performance, which are ranking factors as well.

The primary concept of onsite SEO is making sure your site is totally optimized for search engines to discover. By implementing the right metadata (like descriptions, titles, and alt tags) you ensure that your pages are accessible, readable, and well-linked.

One of the factors Google uses to determine the usefulness and authority of a website is user engagement, or how well your content responds to user queries and intent. As a marketer, you need to understand what users actually need when they ask these questions. Are users trying to learn something, researching or comparing, or are they ready to buy?

When a user searches for a specific term and then clicks on a certain search result, does that user trust the page? Does the page answer their questions? If so, the page provides actual value to users, and Google will rank that page more highly.

Onsite SEO takes a look at the metadata of those pages— the page title, the image alt tags, the meta description—and makes sure they communicate the page value as succinctly as possible on the search engine results page. It also takes a look at your site's design, overall usability, quality of content, and even the technology platform your website was built upon.

Mobile use has also exploded in recent years, so onsite SEO also takes a look at usability. Google has shifted to mobile-first indexing, which essentially means that if a site doesn't display well on a phone, it's not going to rank well for any device. If it's slow, each added second to load will reduce your engagement significantly. Onsite SEO ensures your theme is responsive, usable on various devices, and optimized for accessibility.

BASICS OF OPTIMIZING A SITE FOR SEO

The complexities of SEO are ever-changing, and generally, fairly controversial as many professionals don't agree on which tactics should be employed. We'll try to stay out of the fray and provide a solid rundown of the most dependable, reliable tactics to get your site to a good baseline.

When we first take on a website as a client, there is a straightforward list of things we check out to learn about the current level of optimization. It's surprising how many websites are not optimized at a fundamental level, and it's crucial to make sure these errors are rectified before going on to longer-term, higher-effort tasks.

First, we break the project down into a few sections. While auditing, we're looking at the following:

Meta tags. The title and description have a great deal of influence on click-through rate from the search engine results page, since enticing copy leads to higher engagement from searchers. They let the user know that you have the answer for his query. A user doesn't want to open twenty websites to see which one has the answer: they want to know what the website is about before they even interact with it. Making sure that your meta titles and meta descriptions are unique, descriptive, friendly, and succinct can go a long way in improving the volume of clicks from organic searches. Stripping out auto-generated content from your platform helps make the result look more human and less robot. We also look at images and ensure they all have unique, descriptive alt tags for better accessibility.

On-page content. For a long time, content marketers and SEOs tried to specify an exact "keyword to text" ratio that was ideal for optimized text. For example, they would say that you need 7 keywords per each 100 words of content. So you'd see "best kombucha" and "order kombucha online" sprinkled throughout an article in an attempt to make it feel natural. Now, of course, that's old hat. Search engine algorithms have developed to the point of recognizing far more than just keywords: they're quite good at semantics, intent, and associations. So, it's much more important to write a solid article that solves the user's problems. That doesn't mean that you shouldn't optimize your content, though: having descriptive H2 headings (HTML tags that organize a page) and good markup (alt text on images for screenreaders, for example) throughout goes a long way in making the page readable by search engines (and your users). This is also about usability: not having too many ads, being unique, useful, or educational, being easy to read, having good colors and nice fonts, and providing a pleasant overall experience.

Page speed. In 2018, Google's algorithms went mobile-first, which meant that they started ranking pages based on how well they displayed on mobile. In the end, it's a usability issue, since the majority of web traffic is now flowing through mobile devices. But the latest push has been page speed, which is tangentially related to making sure your site is responsive enough to use on phones. How fast your page loads and how much can display without waiting for heavy JavaScript resources to load definitely affect SEO. At the least, it affects user happiness, and that's what good SEO is all about. Make sure your site isn't burdened by any bloated plugins, make sure your server is fast, and make sure your images aren't large and uncompressed. We usually recommend that a page loads in under three seconds, but the faster, the better!

Internal links. Some of your website pages are more important to your bottom line than others. Sometimes, though, your most important pages don't get the heaviest search engine traffic. Say that you want your kombucha page to get a lot of traffic, because that's where your users actually learn about and ultimately buy the kombucha. But, maybe the most heavily trafficked page on your site is a blog post about the top 10 healthy resolutions for New Year's. That page itself doesn't make you money, but if you naturally link to your kombucha page, you can take advantage of all the traffic being generated on the page about resolutions. That internal link adds a little bit of importance to your kombucha page as well. By adding relevant links, you keep the user interested and convince him to stay longer on your website. It makes you look like a very good source for that specific subject.

Credibility. Search engines and users are both placing increasing importance on credibility and authority. An anonymous site with no verification—like reviews, respectable links, user profiles, or privacy policies, for example—will be viewed as a less trustworthy site. Adding author profiles and real-life contact information, which makes you a real person rather than some back-alley internet marketer, can go a long way toward adding a level of trust in your site. Reviews will also positively influence your conversion rate, so take advantage of them if you're an e-commerce site, a service company, local business, etc.

CASE STUDY: HOW WE INCREASED ORGANIC TRAFFIC BY 88,436 VISITORS (+22%) YEAR OVER YEAR

A large client in the travel industry had a strong background in SEO. A large portion of their clients came from organic traffic from years of successful articles and blog posts. Organic traffic—users naturally visiting your site by finding you through search or external referral—is one of the most powerful and sustainable tools in a marketer's arsenal. It offers a high return on investment and proves to be robust, even considering the whims of algorithms and search technology. Once your site is established as an authority, and others reference it as a reputable source, you're guaranteed great search rankings and referral traffic for years to come.

Yet, developing a strategy that boosts organic traffic in this way (ranking your site through pure merit) isn't something that most digital marketing strategies focus on.

Why is this?

Simply put, because it takes time and effort. It's not just a simple formula: every case is different. If you've frequented enough forums and search blogs, you'll see that a lot of strategies are based on quick-win, low-effort tactics. While these definitely have their place in the right arena, using questionable quality content, which doesn't actually offer your users any real value, won't guarantee your site any success for any long-term period.

That's why we don't recommend or utilize any strategy that relies on gaming the system for success. It's simply not sustainable. We believe that the most solid successes and the most sustainable long-term results come from strategies that focus on quality rather than exploiting loopholes.

We proved this for our client. Our first step was to improve the client's site. We were able to increase organic traffic by over 22% compared to the prior year, through a few carefully researched strategies that focused on improving quality via analytics, keyword research, branding and style updates, and content creation.

The client's old site used an older Wordpress theme which wasn't responsive (it didn't work on mobile devices). The font was ugly and outdated. The design was outdated. The old site's conversion process was dependent upon banner ads—a lot of them. They were bold, brightly colored, and placed everywhere. That seems to make sense, until you take basic human psychology into consideration; we have narrow attention spans, and we're easily distracted. Every extra call-to-action dilutes the power of the others, until eventually, a user just won't know where to click.

So, we put together a truly responsive theme that works on mobile. This step alone boosts Google's opinion of a site. Our next step was removing the banner ads. We added a single call-to-action on each page instead: simple and to the point.

During all of this, we did extensive keyword research to discover which phrases and terms the client "owned" on Google. They ranked #1 for a particular term, but didn't rank at all for another very important category of searches that was in their product offering. Since they had a lot of Google Ads search data history, we were able to identify some important subjects that their users were also interested in. We spent some time creating high-quality media for this category: three 1500-word articles with original photos, detailed content, and high-quality videos.

We embedded a few links from appropriate places throughout the rest of the site to these articles. We added tracking tools. And then we waited.

The results? Just three new articles grew the client's total organic leads by 4.3% in just a few months.[6] For a multi-million dollar company, this was a significant boost for such a relatively low-effort strategy. The traffic kept growing. The site's redesign decreased the bounce rate (how many people leave the site immediately) by 9.11%—that equalled tens of thousands of extra users each year.

Three months in, we started seeing results from the new content. Organic traffic (people coming from Google, Bing, Yahoo, and DuckDuckGo, for example) started slowly increasing. Until eventually, six months later, we saw a 22% year-over-year increase in the number of organic users. This was a total of 88,436 more visitors per year from organic traffic.

CASE STUDY: HOW TO START A SITE FROM SCRATCH & GET TRAFFIC WITHOUT BUILDING ANY BACKLINKS

When I first started in SEO, I kept reading case studies on how to start websites from scratch. They went through all the typical steps: build a site, build links, use social networking to promote it, use advertising, guest post, etc.

Those are all excellent tips—for those of us with a large social presence, a large ad budget, and plenty of experience under our belts. When I first started, I didn't have any of that. None of my followers were interested in the sites I was building, I didn't have the money to advertise, and I didn't have the time or ability to build hundreds of quality backlinks.

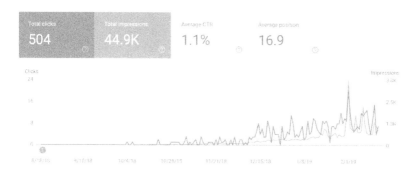

This chart indicates the Google organic search traffic from October to February.

In this case study, I'm going to show you some real numbers and real tactics we used to build a site from scratch and start getting some traffic—without building a single "followed" backlink.

After five months of work, we're getting over 1,250 unique visitors a month, with around 400 of those coming from organic traffic.

I'll first go into a little bit of background on the site. In October 2018, my friend Stu and I decided to launch a new website. We're both massive nerds, and this particular site is dedicated to a specific subset of nerdy 80s nostalgia that we are in love with: cult films and B-movies.

The site is not in a highly commercial niche, which is probably a factor in our quick growth. It does have some competition, in around a dozen established blogs and sites that have been around for 10 or 15 years. At first I wasn't sure the volume or interest was even there, but I was proven wrong.

Originally, I wasn't even thinking about using this site in a case study. I had no idea it was going to be successful. Within a month,

This chart indicates Google image search traffic from the same period.

however, I knew we were on to something, so I started keeping track of our activities.

First, I registered the domain and set up a simple WordPress installation. I spent a few hours modifying a custom theme—I wanted a highly visual, but still clean and simple design that looks a lot like a wiki. WordPress is not an ideal pick, because it's a very slow, bloated CMS, but since both Stu and I were going to be working on content, I decided we needed to use something fairly common.

The site is hosted on a shared hosting package, on a typical Apache server. Nothing fancy at all. It costs $12/mo. The site speed is not terribly impressive, but that's mostly because of two factors.

First, the site is media-intensive. We have a lot of large images (we get over 30% of our traffic from Google Images search—more on that in a minute).

Second, the site is a WordPress site, and WordPress sucks. Even though we are compressing files, have paid lots of attention to optimizing images, and following all the standard best practices for site speed, I have yet to see a WordPress site that doesn't suffer from bloat. It's a real problem and something I hope will someday be fixed.

We are using the standard pack of amazing plugins to track our SEO on the site: Google Analytics and Yoast.

Creating content for the site was the crux of our strategy. And this is where it truly got a little crazy. We created a *lot* of content for the site: 78 individual posts and 5 pages, to be exact. All of this was totally original, exhaustively researched, and written by us.

The content was also in a niche that has almost no existing information out there—some of the topics we wrote about aren't even on Wikipedia. It's truly unexplored territory. Only a handful of blogs, as mentioned above, cover some of these topics.

Each of the posts averaged around 500 words, although some were closer to 1000 words. We created around 10-15 original pictures for each post, keeping them under 300kb each and over 1200px on the shortest side.

Now, an important aside is that we get a huge amount of traffic from Google Images. I'm confident this is because we've spent so much time optimizing these images, keeping alt tags, captions, and metadata within the images in mind. In the first five months, we got over 200 clicks alone from Google Images.

The reality is that this is a whole lot of content, and for most beginning site creators, this strategy only makes sense if you are creating the content yourself. I did the math; if someone came to us at Discosloth and requested a quote for the content marketing done on this project, we would have billed $27,300.

Obviously, that's out of the question for a brand new, unproven site. But you just can't be cheap on content these days. It's got to be original, well-written, researched, and optimized. So, you'll probably have to do that yourself unless you've got a content marketer on staff with some free time.

Over a five-month period, we published 78 posts—so just about one post every other day. We did not worry about timing; it just doesn't matter when you're creating this much content.

Then, we focused on amplifying the content on the site. We created this site from scratch. There was no existing domain, no personal brand equity attached, no existing social handles.

I hooked up Analytics and Google Search Console. After the site was up, Stu went through and created handles at most major social platforms (Pinterest, Tumblr, Twitter, and Google+, rest in peace) and linked them to the site. We also posted on niche Reddit subs whenever we had a piece we thought resonated. Currently, our social following has climbed to 197 followers on Twitter, and 10 followers on Pinterest. Not a whole lot, but something.

I mentioned that we didn't build links. That's true—but that doesn't mean we didn't accumulate them. For a variety of reasons, other folks started linking to the site. Some seem to be automated scrapers, but we're fine with that—it doesn't hurt us. The vast majority seem to be real, valid links—over 150 of them, actually.

As the months went on, we found which sorts of content gained the most traction via organic searches and started focusing on those.

New sites aren't going to rank for high-volume, high-interest keywords. They just simply aren't. So we focused on super-niche topics with almost no volume. We knew we couldn't create one piece that ranks on the first page for 10,000 searches a month, so we created 50 pieces that rank on the first page for 200 searches a month, each.

Looking at the performance so far is where it gets fun—breaking down the traffic we received in the first 5 months.

	Acquisition			Behavior		
	Users ↓	New Users	Sessions	Bounce Rate	Pages / Session	Avg. Session Duration
	2,849	2,849	3,630	78.37%	1.98	00:02:21
1 ■ Direct	1,267			83.54%		
2 ■ Organic Search	738			74.76%		
3 ■ Social	459			77.63%		
4 Referral	447			71.28%		

Most of the "direct" visits should be attributed to social and organic.

It's worth noting that Google Analytics does not always do a great job of reporting channels, and that's why you see so many "direct" visits. That's because Safari, one of our highest-volume, highest-performing browsers, recently introduced some privacy features which block a lot of personally identifiable information from Analytics. From doing some dives into the data and watching day-to-day, I can tell that a large percentage of those "direct" visits are actually correlated with posts on Reddit, and another large percentage is correlated to spikes in organic traffic. Absent a better data set, I'd say that most of the "direct" visits need to be assigned to either organic or referral categories.

Organic traffic is our Shangri-La, because it's so hard to get and so valuable to keep. We were very pleased with such a wide range of search engines. Obviously, Google is the largest with 635 visits, but that's followed by:
- Bing (58)
- Yahoo (27)
- DuckDuckGo (14)
- Yandex (16)

- ✦ Seznam (4)
- ✦ AOL, Ask, Baidu, and Ecosia (1 each)

Traffic from social platforms:
- ✦ Reddit (256)
- ✦ Facebook (172)
- ✦ Tumblr (47)
- ✦ Pinterest (18)
- ✦ Twitter (7)

Referrals are a little trickier for me to report right now, without majorly revealing the domain of our site, but traffic referred from non-social-media sites is 378 in total.

We also added a newsletter signup on the site a few weeks ago —we've gotten 15 signups so far.

The engagement across the board looks pretty good. The average time on page from all channels is well over two minutes. Some of that is probably skewed by some outliers we've noticed— there seem to be quite a few no-life nerds who have spent hours on the site, reading 15-20 pages. I'm not talking about myself. No, not at all.

Demographics are equally awesome, since we have the majority coming from tech-forward countries (the United States leads the pack at 69%, followed by Canada at 5%, the UK at 4%, Germany at 2.7%, Australia at 1.9%, and Ukraine at 1.7%).

The majority of users are males, aged 25-44, which fits in with our assumption that only the nerdiest of neckbeards actually want to read about the sort of geeky crap we're writing about.

Now, deciding the future is next up on the agenda. We're going to keep on keeping on. We will maintain the same content plan (it gets exhausting publishing 3-4 articles a week, but it's all in the name of science).

We haven't actively built links or pushed for traffic from external sites, but I'm considering reaching out to others in the niche and doing some cross-promotion. This could increase our ongoing referral traffic quite a bit.

So what are the steps to take when you're trying to improve your organic traffic? Let's boil them down into a few concise points.

1. Focus on quality content that people will find useful, bookmark, and share naturally with friends.

2. Remove distracting banner ads and focus on single calls-to-action.

3. Redesign your site so it doesn't look like it's selling something...use a design language that conveys it's there to be valuable.

4. Research keywords (whether short- or long-tail) that you don't own yet, and focus on those.

5. Be honest and upfront in your messaging, and treat your users like people rather than numbers.

Almost always, if you focus on creating value and usability for your audience, this will boost your organic traffic massively.

PAY-PER-CLICK ADVERTISING

""A good advertisement is one which sells the product without drawing attention to itself." – David Ogilvy

Although we'd all like to get free attention for our brands, it's not always possible. Especially if you're in a highly competitive or tech-focused industry! That's where paid advertising comes in. Pay-per-click (PPC) advertising is one of the most economical ways to advertise in the digital world, but if you don't know how to structure your campaigns, it can be extremely costly. We'll cover some of the basics on building a profitable PPC strategy.

Whether you're a small business owner, a marketing professional brushing up on digital techniques, or a student, this chapter will serve as a comprehensive resource for understanding the strategy behind profitable pay-per-click campaigns.

PPC stands for "pay-per-click." It means that the advertiser pays only when someone clicks directly on the ad. It's an easy way of getting users to your website without waiting for your website to become visible organically.

PPC advertising is the way in which companies display their ads in search engines and other platforms. The most effective ads are shown when a user is searching for their products or services, or for other closely related search queries. The most popular PPC providers, or channels, are search and social networks like Google, Bing, Baidu, Yandex, Facebook, and Instagram.

In a nutshell, advertisers bid in an auction for ad placement. Your position in the searches is based on your bid (how much you're willing to pay for a click), on your ads, and your website's relevancy (also known as Quality Score).

Google and the other leading search engines have an automated algorithm that is basically an invisible auction. The higher your bid, the higher your position in the searches.

This chapter isn't about which buttons to click or which interface panels to open. It's not going to tell you specific processes, like how to filter data by campaign name, for example. You can just Google things like that. Rather, this is like playing baseball. Anyone can pick up a bat and learn how to hit a ball. But how do you win a game? Technical skill alone gets you nowhere. Strategy and psychology are the crucial elements behind a winning team.

WHAT CHANNELS ARE AVAILABLE FOR PPC?

Search engines include PPC ads embedded into their results page: for example, someone searching for "organic kombucha" would see paid results for places that sell kombucha. Google is one of the largest search engines. Bing is a significant second player, mostly within the United States. Other search engines like DuckDuckGo are built on top of other engines, but also offer advertising. Yandex is the largest search engine for Russian speakers, reaching hundreds of millions of users worldwide. Baidu is the primary search engine for the Chinese market.

Most social platforms also offer PPC ads, but we'll cover these in the social media chapter since the strategy is vastly different. Ads on platforms like Facebook, Instagram, or LinkedIn are really only targetable via interest, not queries: for example, on Facebook, you could only target people who are *interested* in organic foods, but not necessarily actively searching to buy kombucha. Whereas with platforms like a search engine, you can easily reach the person at the exact moment they need the product the most. You can use platforms like Quora or Twitter a little more easily to target intent and queries, since users can search a hashtag or look at a specific question.

WHO NEEDS TO KNOW ABOUT PAID ADVERTISING?

Knowing the basics of PPC is important to every marketer, whether you're a small business owner, a marketing strategist, or want to be a PPC specialist, specifically. If you're spending money on PPC, you need to know how paid advertising works and how your campaign should look. This section will guide you through the process of creating a campaign from scratch, but most of all, it will help you understand the logic behind it. Setting up campaigns is not just clicking different buttons and adding the first few relevant keywords that come to your mind. It's about research and understanding your customer's struggles and needs.

It's important to understand that PPC (as with any other type of marketing) cannot be wholly learned by reading a book or watching tutorials. It's a very hands-on process. Tutorials will help you avoid making some major mistakes, but the goal of this guide is to give you enough knowledge so that when you start working with something like Google Ads, you can just as easily figure it out on your own without wasting money.

To be clear, the fact that you've created an account and created a good campaign doesn't guarantee you will get sales. There are lots of things to consider before you decide to invest in paid ads. Do you have an existing brand? If no one has ever heard of you, they might not want to spend their money on your website. The internet is full of scammers and low quality products. How can you set yourself apart from them? There are a few common reasons why even the best PPC campaign won't work for you:

First, if your website has bad grammar, empty sections, low quality images, or low quality content, you're going to have a hard time converting into sales.

Next, if someone searches for your brand and they see bad reviews about you on other websites, that's also a very difficult situation from which to see success.

If your website is hard to navigate, this also reduces your success. There are too many options online for users to spend time figuring out how to use your website.

Low page-loading speed is another consideration. Each second you keep a user waiting increases the chance they'll leave your site for greener pastures.

And last but not least, if your website is not optimized for mobile, you'll be sacrificing a lot of potential sales. You can use many online tools, including Google's Mobile-Friendly Test, to check this. Also, make sure you check your mobile speed. Some people forget how important is for websites to be optimized for mobile: in 2018, 52.2% of website traffic worldwide was generated through mobile phones, up from 50.3% the previous year.

I'M DOING SEO—DO I STILL NEED TO SPEND ON PAID?

To get the best conversion rates (how many people complete your desired goal, like purchasing or contacting you) and increase your brand trust, you need visibility on all channels that make sense for your business model. If you have good paid campaigns and no SEO, users might not trust you, as your online presence is limited to ads. If you do only SEO and no paid advertising, it might take you a lot longer (possibly years) to get in front of your clients.

The first thing that's important to keep in mind is that users won't necessarily see you online once and buy right away. Just use your own browsing habits as a reference. Do you ever click on an ad and make a purchase without any further research? For a brand you've never heard about? The answer is most likely no!

We'll talk about this in a later chapter, but it's important to understand the idea of multi-channel attribution. In short, it helps you see all the channels that users use before they convert on your website.

Beyond giving you visibility on multiple channels, SEO helps you create a brand and be useful, informative, and educational. Let's look at two scenarios.

Let's say someone comes to your website via an ad. He's never heard of you before. All you have on the website is a landing page with a big button saying "Buy Now" and some bullet points saying how awesome you are.

The second scenario: someone comes to your website via an ad. He's also never heard of you before. He gets to your website and can see the product he's searched for. He sees an entire page describing benefits in detail, maybe even a link to some studies supporting your claims about your product. You also have a blog section where you explain how to use it, or who it won't work for. Then, the user Googles your brand and can see other people writing about their experiences of buying the same product from you. This is all a part of SEO!

Can you see how those differences could increase your conversion rate? Can you also see why a good paid campaign is not always enough to get good results?

The third thing to consider is how paid advertising can help your SEO efforts. Paid advertising can help you quickly test specific keywords, phrases, audiences, or even business ideas. Once you see what works, you can do more SEO around it, creating content and so on, already having confirmed that there is demand for the idea.

Types Of PPC Ads

What are paid search ads? Search advertising ads are placed within a search engine's results page. They have a similar format as organic results (which are unpaid), are usually on the top (first 3-4 results), and sometimes a few are on the bottom of the results.

Search ads work based on the search term entered into the search engine. The most popular search engines are Google, Bing, Yandex, Baidu, Yahoo, and DuckDuckGo.

The benefit of search ads is that you can respond directly to someone's issues, questions, or needs; as opposed to social media advertising, you don't have to convince your audience that they need detox juices: they already know that and are looking for some to buy.

What are display ads? Display ads (or display advertising) is a form of online advertising on websites or apps that use image ads, rich media ads, video ads, or text ads. Google's display advertising reaches 80% of global internet users. Display ads catch users whenever they are surfing online but not searching for a specific product or service. Because of this, the main goal of display advertising should not be getting clicks, but to drive brand awareness.

There are multiple ways you can target users via display advertising. One of the most important is remarketing. Remarketing is used for websites that want to remind previous users about themselves. It can target users that visited a specific product on your website but didn't purchase, and essentially follow them around the internet showing them the exact product they were interested in. You can target users based on their interests and habits, what they're actively researching, or how they've interacted with your business.

What are shopping ads? Shopping ads show more detailed information about the product you sell. Usually shopping ads contain an image, price, brand, title, and link directly to the item in your store. These ads are shown on top of search engines. Shopping ads are not available in all countries, so check the relevant availability before you start. Most shopping ads are created on Google, although Bing has an option for them, too.

This type of ads works very well, as it gives your audience a visual representation of the product before they click. The downside is that you cannot target specific keywords. Google will choose which search queries you ads will appear for, based on the product description and title.

What are video ads? Video ads (or video advertising) are mainly used as YouTube ads. They appear when someone is searching or watching a YouTube video. Instead of per click, you pay for each view.

Same as display ads, the greatest benefit of running YouTube ads is not in getting clicks or sales. It's about brand awareness— possibly annoying people that just want to listen to some music.

It's very important to execute video ads correctly, as users ignore most ads on YouTube. You want to make sure you create something that will catch their attention in the first 2 seconds. The approach is different than TV ads. Since they're skippable (unlike TV ads) they need to be catchy, funny, smart, and speak to a user's emotions more than anything else. A common fault of YouTube advertisers is going into too much detail or making a video too long.

Say a client is thinking about a YouTube campaign. They already have a 30-second TV spot produced, but this video wouldn't do well on YouTube. They might need a short, 15-second, inspirational ad with a primary focus on branding rather than sales. Views are extremely cheap and highly targetable on YouTube, which means someone who sees a video will also likely see some search ads later on, as well! You can also target users that have already visited your website (remarketing), based on specific interests, or even just a specific channel.

How The Way We Search Changed

One of the most important parts of any online marketing campaign is keyword research. If you know who your audience is and how they search for your service, 80% of your work is done.

Google's continual algorithm updates, together with the technology used to interpret our search results, has caused the way we've actually used search in the past few years to drastically change.

In 2006 we used keywords to search for information (like typing in *organic juice*); in today's world, we ask questions and actually talk to the search engine. Our searches now look more like "where can I buy organic juice?"

As search changes, the way to create campaigns and the way we do our research changes too. We don't just target our product's name, but we target people's questions about what we can offer. This will only continue to be important as voice search becomes more common. The research helps you create useful content for your user, but it also helps you choose the right keywords to target for your paid campaigns.

If you're a lawyer with a focus on gender discrimination, you'd probably think about targeting *gender discrimination lawyer,* but what you should actually target are searches like, *I got fired for being pregnant.*

WHERE TO START WITH KEYWORD RESEARCH

Say we're a creating a campaign for a website that sells different types of organic juices. As a small company just now entering the world of PPC, the client's initial budget is $2,000 per month, targeting the United States market. The juices on the website are separated into a few categories: Cleanse Packs, Cold Pressed Juices, Organic Soft Drinks, and Organic Kombucha.

Google Ads would probably have great potential for this site: you can target people actively searching to order some organic kombucha to have delivered to their doors.

Before we start researching the keywords, we want to have a better understanding of our audience. Who are the people buying these products? What else are they interested in? Where do we find these people hanging out? And very importantly, what are the reasons they are buying this product?

First, create a document with a column for your main products, and a column for all negative keywords you can find. Update this list throughout the research process.

The first tool to use in creating a Google Ads campaign is the Google Keyword Planner. It's totally free, and it's an excellent way to start your research. Just make sure you use it in an active account with payment details already set up, otherwise the suggestions you'll get will be very broad. The Keyword Planner helps generate ideas on how users search, and it gives you some phrasing variations that you might not have thought about. It also can be a good resource for negative keywords. Let's start with researching how people are searching for cold pressed juices. We find that some users search for *cold press juicer*. As we are selling juices, not machines, we don't want to appear for anyone searching for juicers, so it goes into our Negative Keywords column.

Juice cleanse diet and *juice cleanse weight loss* are good keywords, but users might be more interested in information rather than buying a specific product. So the conversion rate will be lower for those searches. For now, we'll wait since those searches seem like they are from people looking for educational information rather than purchasing something.

If we have a bigger budget, we might want to create a separate ad group for those, so we can track the performance separately and limit the budget for it. Most PPC providers, like Google, let you separate your account into campaigns and ad groups. A campaign is the overarching container for structuring your campaign. An ad group is a smaller subset in which you place your actual ads.

We also notice that users are searching for *3 day juice cleanse.* Make sure there is an applicable product for this search, and add these keywords to the Juice Cleanse ad group.

Once you've got your ideas in the Keywords Planner, Google them! First, look at Google Auto Suggest. It's a great place to search for inspiration and to see what people are searching for. If you're searching for ideas, use an asterisk to get ideas for unknown or variable words. For example, search ** kombucha* and you'll find other words that commonly appear before kombucha. Or, just use a letter, A through Z, and see what Google suggests. In this case, you could search *kombucha a* and see what words start with A that commonly follow kombucha.

Now, we have even more info to add to our sheet. You'll see a lot of irrelevant terms—perhaps something like *kombucha vape,* or *kombucha recipes.* We know that we don't want to appear for *vape, recipes, whole foods,* or any specific locations that we are not targeting. On the other hand, we can also learn some other common words that these organic kombucha hippies use, like *organic fruit juice, juice cleanse delivery,* and more.

By the end of this exercise, you'll have an amazing list of negatives (this is very, very important) as well as different variations on how users search. Even if you can't use every single suggestion as a keyword, make sure your website answers the main questions users ask. Identifying these common questions specific to your product is so crucial, because it will help with both your organic traffic, and your user trust and retention. Once someone clicks on your ad, based on what info they find on your website, they'll decide if they can trust you or not.

Some other resources for keyword research:

Bing Keyword Planner. Bing is a thing! And it can give you some additional insights on what you're searching for. You can find the Bing Keyword Planner within the Bing Ads interface. It's definitely worth trying out.

Answer the Public. This is a very useful website, and we really like the design (maybe this part isn't helpful for your research...but we still like it a lot). As they say, "Enter your keyword and he'll suggest content ideas in seconds"—you'll get valuable results with actionable information.

Research your existing audience. If you already have existing traffic, we start with Google Analytics data. If you go to the Audience tab, you can learn more about your demographics. For example, for Anya's Organic Juices, we might see that our main audience are women aged 25-34. You might have noticed that you might only see data for, say, 51% of the total audience. The reason for this is that Google Analytics can see demographics only if users have already shared it with them, in their Gmail account for example. In your Audience tab, you can see what your users are interested in. In the same place, you can find info about which devices your users use, their behavior, and of course, their geolocation. If your website's main audience are women aged 25-34, that doesn't necessarily mean that they are the best quality audience, or that you need to create campaigns to target them! While this *might* be the case, you need to look at engagement and conversion rates to see which audience actually has the best quality.

Even though women aged 25-34 are the most common visitors, they might not be the most profitable visitors. We can look at the metrics and realize we actually want to target women aged 35-54, as they are far more likely to purchase your product.

Google Search Console. This tool is used to track your organic searches. If you have it linked to your Google Analytics account, then you can see the results directly there.

Google Analytics Site Search. If your website has a search option using Google's site search functionality, you can see what people searched for in your Analytics account. Based on this data, you'll be able to see how people search and what they need from you. Use this to discover which problems your audience is trying to solve. When you've found these problems, tailor your ads to help solve them!

There are many other tools that can be used, some of which are free, like the ones mentioned above. You can also use paid tools (like Moz Keyword Explorer or SEMRush) and you can always get creative! Keep in mind that this data is informational, and you should not base your decision on data only, as it might show you only half of the picture.

BUILDING A PPC CAMPAIGN

Nail down your primary goal. Is it more website traffic? Is it sales? Do you want someone to download your app? Or is it brand awareness and increasing visibility?

The campaign will look very different depending upon the goal. It'll target different keywords, use different PPC channels, and there will be totally different types of metrics to watch. Before you start a campaign, make sure you have these questions answered:

+ What is my goal (why do I need PPC?)
+ What is my monthly budget (how much am I willing to spend to accomplish my goal?)

- If my goal is sales, how much can I spend and still be profitable (what is the cost per acquisition?)
- Where does my target audience live?
- What age and gender are my ideal audience? (these are some of the most common demographics you're able to target)
- What topics are my ideal audience interested in?
- What is the socioeconomic demographic of my ideal audience?
- Does my product require the user to do a lot of research before purchase, or is it an impulse buy?

Only after you have answers to all of these questions can you start setting up your PPC campaign. If you do it before you know these answers, you'll incur a lot of expense for little to no revenue.

CHOOSING THE RIGHT PPC CHANNEL

Different channels work for different niches. We've seen clients who spent $60,000 a month on Facebook ads and got an ROI of 125%, but Google Ads just wouldn't work for them. We've seen other clients spend $30,000 a month on Google Ads with an ROI of 50%, but months of Facebook ads just wouldn't bring any sales.

The main difference between these two clients was that the first had a low cost product that many people would see on Facebook and purchase on impulse without researching. The second client had a high cost product which people researched on Google for months before purchasing.

In the end, even if only one channel works for you, it doesn't mean you need to ignore the others. If a company is doing amazingly on Google, but doesn't have a presence on Facebook, the company might not have a lot of trust. And trust is 99.99% of sales (that's a made up number, but we'll stake our reputation on it). Test extensively. Patience is a virtue, since you shouldn't expect too many sales at the beginning as you spend to build your brand. Good upfront branding will pay back many times in the end! Start with Instagram if you're selling fashion. Facebook if you're selling funny t-shirts. Google Ads if you're selling trips to luxury resorts in Africa. And don't forget about Bing Ads if you're targeting the US.

How To Advertise For Branding & Awareness

Historically, branding has always been one of the most complicated types of campaigns to track. It takes a longer time to show results, and it's difficult to associate specific results with the campaign. A branding campaign will create awareness, and people will know your name, but it doesn't necessarily bring you immediate sales.

For a branding campaign, it's recommended to test many options and determine which brings you better results. You can usually start with a display campaign on Google. The Custom Intent audience allows you to make a list of keywords your perfect customer uses. Based upon this list, you'll have an audience that is actively researching using the keywords you picked. Or, if you've got a list of websites that use Google AdSense and have a high volume of traffic, you can create an audience which only includes users visiting these websites. If you'd rather target users based on their interests and habits, you can create an Affinity Audience. For an organic juice store, this would give us options like "Green Living Enthusiasts" and "Health and Fitness Buffs." Your ads need to be memorable, but not too pushy. You're not trying to annoy your users! Have a clear message, use short sentences, and explain the top benefits of your service.

Video advertising is an excellent strategy for affordably raising awareness about your products. You can additionally select specific YouTube channels you want to appear on, or choose which topics and keywords you'd like to appear for. Continue by choosing location, budgets, and bidding. For a video you bid per view (CPV) and on average, bids cost a few cents. For a branding ad, you'll be able to select in-stream video format ads. In-stream ads are the videos that play before, during, and after another video. Users have the option to skip an ad after 5 seconds. Make sure your video has a single main call-to-action. Don't forget that you're targeting users who have no idea who you are. Get their attention in the first 5 seconds (before they can skip). Don't use too much noise or annoyance—that's not how you want to get their attention.

All major search engines support search campaigns: ads which appear in the SERPs (search engine results page). For branding campaigns, you don't want to target highly specific keywords or phrases. Target users searching for information and ideas—people who are still in the research phase rather than ready to purchase.

For our fictional Anya's Organic Juices branding campaign, we'll target users searching for *detox juice diet* and *benefits of cold pressed juices*, rather than users searching for *where to buy organic juices near me*. Doing this will allow you to target a much broader audience. The CPC for general terms is usually cheaper, as well. You'll be the first brand they see during their research. Even if your audience is not ready to buy right away, when they are ready, they'll have you in mind and likely go directly to your website.

Your goal for a branding campaign is to get as much website traffic and visibility as possible.

CAMPAIGNS FOR INCREASING SALES

If you're already in the market and your website and brand is trustworthy, you probably want to focus on making sales. You should use a sales-focused strategy, rather than branding alone.

When creating a sales-focused search campaign, focus on searches that indicate an interest in purchasing your product. Your campaign should be specific and well-structured. The setup itself is similar to search campaigns for branding purposes, but you want to focus on conversion and leads rather than on website traffic. From the beginning, you pick a different goal: sales if you have an ecommerce website, or leads if you have a service-based website.

For an organic juice company, we want users searching for "buy organic juices online" or "the best place to buy organic cold pressed juices."

Shopping campaigns show great results for e-commerce and retail websites. The primary benefit is that users see the product images, price, and description before clicking. This means you only pay for clicks from users who know what to expect. Another huge benefit of a shopping campaign is that your product data is always updated instantly. The main limitation is that shopping campaigns are not available in all countries.

Remarketing campaigns allow you to show your ads to a defined set of users who've already visited your site. You can separate users based on their behavior (converters vs non-converters), specific pages they've visited on your site, the specific regions they're from, how many pages they've visited, or amount of time they've spent reading your articles.

CAMPAIGN STRUCTURE AND NAMING

Now that you know what sort of campaigns you need and how to set them up, you need to think more about your account structure. It's important to do it correctly, since the more organized the campaign, the better—we'll be able to optimize later on.

While doing keyword research, you've already completed half of the job! First, decide what type of campaign to create. Say you want a shopping campaign, a search campaign, and a dynamic remarketing campaign. You'll want to keep them all separate, and each will have a separate budget.

Also, if you want to create a campaign with brand searches only (for searches like *anya's organic juices*), you'll want to separate it from the main search campaign. The reason is that a brand campaign will always be many times more successful compared to non-brand campaigns, for the simple fact that if someone searches directly for your brand name, they're already much more likely to convert compared to a general researcher.

If you've got a product that you want to attract more attention, and it has a separate budget, you'll also want a separate campaign.

The campaign names should be short and clear. It's like creating product category on your website. Never use names that are too generic like "Campaign 1," or it will be a nightmare to remember which campaign does what. Now that you have a campaign, you need to name your ad groups. The ad group name should represent the keywords targeted within it. In the "Pressed Juice" ad groups, you want only keywords containing the words *pressed* and *juice*, like *+buy +organic +pressed +juice* or *+pressed +juice +delivery*.

Besides helping you track everything better, it will also help improve your Quality Score and relevancy. In the end, the better your campaign is organized, the less you'll pay for your clicks and the higher your revenue will be.

ADS & EXTENSIONS

The ad itself is very important, as this is the first thing the user sees before interacting with you. Whether we're talking about social media ads, search, or display, all ads should follow some of the same rules. Here's an important one: be respectful to the users. Additionally, have appealing visuals, a clear message, good grammar, quality images, and a clear call-to-action.

You'd think it goes without saying, but just remember the pushy, in-your-face ads from ten or twenty years ago. You know, like the late-night infomercials telling you to call now, and get *two* for $19.95! Some advertisers are still trying to use those old techniques, but thankfully they're now forbidden on most advertising platforms. Make sure you spell correctly and use correct grammar, don't use too many exclamation points, don't write in all caps, don't use emojis, and don't use phrases like "click here." Your ads will likely be disapproved if you do this!

In the ads, use the wording your audience uses to search for your service. Looking at your search terms report, you might see that users like the phrase "Best Organic Remedy Kombucha," so why not use it as your title?

As you can see in the example above, the actual ad text is only half of the job (or even less). To make your ad stand out and have more visibility, you need to create ad extensions. These are some of the types of extensions available now:

- Sitelink extension—Show additional links from your website
- Callout extension—Add more benefits of your products
- Structured snippet extension—Add specifics of your products (brand names, destinations)
- Call extension—Your phone number
- Message extension—Let people text you directly from the ad
- Location extension—Show your business info (address, working hours)
- Affiliate location extension—Show affiliate location
- Price extension—Show prices of your products and services
- App extension—Add a link to your app
- Promotion extension—Used just for special offers

KEYWORD MATCH TYPES

Keyword Match Types help control which searches your ads will appear for. These tell Google how flexible you want to be.

A keyword is the word you choose to target in your Ads account. A search term includes the exact words or phrases the customer enters while searching on a search engine. Keywords and search terms are different: don't confuse them! There are 5 main types of keywords:

Broad match. Ads will show for for synonyms, misspellings, and related searches. So, if your keyword is "organic juices," your ads could show for "buy cold pressed juices." Symbol: no symbols added

Broad match modifier. These ads will show only for searches that include one or more keywords (or close variations, no matter the order). So, if your keyword is "+organic +juice +delivery", your ads will appear for the search term *home delivery organic juice*. Symbol: Plus sign, for example: +keyword

Phrase match. These ads will show only for searches that match a phrase (or close variations). It might still include words before and after the phrase you target. So, if your keyword is *"detox juice delivery"*, your ads will appear for searches like *best detox juice delivery california*. Symbol: "keyword"

Exact match. Ads will show on searches that include the exact words or phrases you're targeting (or close variations). So if your keyword is [buy organic juice], your ad will appear for someone searching *buy organic juices*. Symbol: [keyword]

Negative match. Ads will show on searches that don't include negative keywords. If you sell organic juice, but you don't do wholesale orders, you'll add the keyword "-wholesale" as a negative, and if someone searches for *wholesale organic juices*, your ads won't show up. Symbol: -keyword

Because broad match keywords don't give you much control over which searches you appear for, we usually don't recommend unless you have very low search volume or a very limited niche.

BUDGETS & BIDDING

As we've established, online advertising works on the principle that you pay when someone clicks on your ad (pay-per-click), and acquiring such ads is based on auctions. Let's say that five companies want to appear for the search term "organic juices delivery." Each company will bid on this keyword. A bid is the maximum amount you are willing to pay for a click. Those who pay more get higher positions. The higher your position on a search engine, the more people will see your ad.

Decisions about how much you want to spend for a click is not totally up to you. Since your competitors are already there, they have already established an average of how much it costs to be on top of the search results.

Your cost per click has to be competitive for people to see your ads. While doing keyword research, you can usually get an idea of how much a click should cost for your keywords. As our CPC (cost-per-click) is different based on the bids of our competitors, in the exact moment someone searches, our CPC will vary as well.

There are also different strategies for bidding. You can choose between manually bidding or automated bidding. Manually bidding per ad group or even per each keyword, based on their importance to us, can more thoroughly analyze each keyword's performance and choose the best bids for each—this takes more time, but the effort can save a lot of money.

On the other side of the coin are automated bidding strategies developed by the search engine's software. The main benefit is that you won't need to choose your bids. The downside is that you won't be able to control your CPC and, based on our past experience with these strategies, a click that should cost $2 can turn into $15. You can still chose the maximum you want to pay, or you can choose how much you want to pay for conversion (completion of your goal). Overall, we don't generally recommend this method. Use it only if you have a large number of campaigns, and you don't have someone monitoring performance of the campaigns regularly.

If you decide to use a manual bidding strategy, you can add an option of a bid adjustment based on device, location, audience, demographics, and even household income (for US only).

If you've decided that you want to bid higher for users that have already visited your website, you can import your audience from Analytics (as we previously discussed in the remarketing section) and add a bid adjustment of +30% to make sure that you appear on top for all users that are already familiar with your business.

Also, if you're targeting a bigger country like the US, some areas might be more competitive than others. With the same bid, you might be the first position in Arkansas, but only the fourth for California. In this case, you add bid adjustment to make sure you have a good position even in more competitive areas.

Don't forget that when you set up a new campaign, you assume which bidding strategy and CPC are the best for you, but you never know for sure. Once the campaign has some clicks, make sure you update and optimize based on performance, conversion rate, and average position. Also, don't forget that you can lower your CPC by having a high Quality Score. The better the user experience is and the more closely targeted your campaign is, the lower your CPC will be.

Monthly Budgets

Now that we know the approximate cost per click, we'll need to decide our monthly budget.

Let's say that Anya's Organics estimated CPC is $2.50. We must calculate the amount we can spend in order for a sale to be profitable. If your average revenue per conversion is $100, but your built-in overhead (besides advertising expenses) is $40. Your margin = revenue − expenses, or $60.

Now that we know the margin, we know how much we can spend on advertising per order. If our average CPC is $2.50, we need to make a sale every 24 clicks to break even (24 * 2.50 = 60).

However, Anya's Organics wants to turn a profit (don't we all?), so they decide they need to make a sale every 20 clicks (for a $10 profit per sale).

So, we want to spend a maximum of $50 on advertising per sale. This might not happen right away, as it's a competitive niche. We'll need to test the campaign, see what works best, and then work on getting the desired cost per conversion.

It's also essential to understand our desired conversion rate. To calculate it, divide conversions by the number of interactions with your ad. To get a sale every 20 clicks we need a conversion rate of 5%. In the end, you will also want to know your ROI.

How many sales a month do you want to make? Say you want to start with 10 sales per month. If your cost per sale is around $50, your monthly budget should be $50 * 10 = $500/mo.

PPC Management & Optimization

Now your campaign is ready to go. Congrats! But it's not over yet; actually, the most important part of the job starts now.

When you create a campaign, you first create the foundation. This foundation is based on our research, on our ideas of how people search, and hopefully on some existing data (which isn't always available with new websites). We don't know exactly what will work and give us sales. So, where do we start? We get this question a lot. And it's not an easy answer.

There is no way that anyone has a perfect campaign the first day, or even the first week, after setup! Once you have a running campaign, patience is a virtue. It might require a few days or a few months after the campaign starts (based on volume and budget) to gather enough data to have a cursory idea of how the campaign is performing. In many cases, this makes it even more important to know how to keep your campaign optimized in the meantime. Here are a few pro tips:

Find the average cost-per-click for keywords. Since you don't know what bidding strategy your competitors use, you'll still need to adjust bidding based upon how much competition there is, and the average position you want to maintain.

Targeted keywords have been set up, but remember: keywords are not necessarily search terms. Just because the word *kombucha* is a keyword that is relevant to your business does not mean it's a word you'll need to try to appear for. For example, you's rather appear for the search term *buy kombucha online* instead! You must constantly monitor the search term report. See which terms you appear for, which aren't correct (add these as negative keywords), and determine which ones you want to target more specifically. Once you find these, add them as a keyword. You can now adjust bids for it and track it separately from others.

At the beginning, you set up 2 or 3 ads to test wording variations. Once you gather data, see which have better click-through-rate (CTR) and better conversion rates. Pause the ones that perform poorly, and create new variations to get even better performance. Find specific phrases searchers use. Use these to adjust the ad text.

Looking at the keyword view, track your Quality Score. A score of 7-10 means users find your ads relevant to the keywords, and they find your landing page useful. If you have a low Quality Score, see what's missing in each area; if ad relevance is bringing your average down, try updating your ad wording. Make sure it's highly relevant to the keywords you're targeting. If you're targeting users searching for *kombucha*, you don't want ads saying *best organic juices* sending traffic to a general page. You want these users to see an ad saying *best organic kombucha,* which sends them to a specialized kombucha drink page.

We'll talk more about how to use Google Analytics in another chapter, but for this point in the process, a valuable Analytics feature for optimization is tracking user engagement. Compare bounce rate, time on page, and pages per session with the other channels that bring traffic to your site (like organic search, social, or direct traffic); you can even compare between all campaigns and ad groups. Do users searching for "juice cleanse" have higher engagement compared to those that searched for "pressed juices?"

Check your performance per device. Do users that came from a mobile device have a better conversion rate, CTR or engagement? Or do users on desktop computers perform better?

While targeting mobile, make sure your website is easy to use from a mobile device. Is it easy to read and easy to purchase? If desktop has a higher conversion rate, maybe you need to add a bid adjustment for it, or perhaps you want to lower mobile bids by, say, 15%? While optimizing the campaign, asking yourself questions is the best you can do!

If the website is just not that great, you might want to work on improving the look, usability, or wording. Even the best campaign can't help a crappy website. If that's the case, see if there's something uniquely appealing in your offer, ads or anything else which might need to be changed. See what the competitors offer for their products. Do they have a better offer for pressed juices compared to you? Or is it something else?

Online advertising has amazing benefits compared to traditional media. It allows you to see nearly everything that's happening on your site and within your ad campaigns. You should take advantage of this feature, and gather as much as data as you can before making advertising decisions.

Social Media Marketing

"Our job is to connect to people, to interact with them in a way that leaves them better than we found them." – Seth Godin

Users spend more of their time on social media than anywhere else on the internet. The sheer amount time spent on platforms like Facebook, Instagram, and Twitter has skyrocketed, and it shows no signs of slowing. Yet at the same time, social media marketing has proven difficult in terms of return on investment (ROI): users often just aren't interested in spending money while they're on Facebook. So how do you take advantage of the user base on these platforms and create a quality strategy?

If any one niche within the greater world of digital marketing changes every single day, it's social media.

From the bulletin boards of the 1980s to the forums, Tripods, and GeoCities of the early 2000s, all the way to the MySpace of 2005, and the Facebook of 2012, and the Periscope of 2016—new mediums are coming and going as swiftly as the seasons change.

That's why it's probably not very helpful to dwell on any specific social media channel for too long. Platforms and the strategies that go along with them change too fast, die too fast, and are born too fast.

Theory is important in social media marketing, though—as long as you understand how it works, you'll be able to adapt your ideas and strategies to new platforms as they come along.

Whether it's through Twitter, Pinterest, LinkedIn, or Instagram —in the end, people are social animals, and there are ways to reach them everywhere.

THE DEATH OF ORGANIC REACH

At one time, it was actually pretty easy to market on social media. Things could easily be shared, cool stuff got a lot of traction, and the users were usually forward-thinking early adopters. But, things change fast, and with the proliferation of smartphones and iPads came a mass migration of older users and younger users, technologically savvy users and technologically ignorant users, people with money and people with no money. Billions of people are using social media now, and the companies have monetized their platforms in response.

Now, we could harp on the benefits or downsides of this all day long, but in the end we just want to know how to market with them. So, here's why all of this matters: social platforms are consistently making it harder to reach an audience without paying for it. That's why almost every social platform worth it's salt has an advertising platform now. Say our imaginary client, Anya's Organic Juices, wants to reach potential juice fans on Facebook. If they post a status update, guess what?

Nobody's gonna see it.

Facebook knows that Anya's Organics is just a regular ol' company. Facebook's algorithm will ensure that nobody will see this status—if they don't see it, they can't share it. What does Anya's Organics do if they want people to see it? Pay to boost the post. Same with Twitter, LinkedIn, Instagram, and the rest. If you're a business, you can almost guarantee that any outbound links are going to be dampened unless you're paying to boost their reach.

The reality of today is that it's almost impossible to see significant social growth unless you're paying for it. There is still the possibility of finding small niches that can grow organically, but the tradeoff is extreme amounts of hands-on time and community building.

That hands-on time required to grow a social community is not just an hour here and there—it's usually a full-time job, so in the end, it still costs a lot to grow a social community, whether it takes paying an hourly employee or spending your own time.

That said, there's definitely a benefit to keeping your social media properties alive: if a potential customer is researching a business, then they want to see that the company is active online.

And there's still the huge benefit of using social platforms in order to advertise. There are some specific types of content which work best for each platform; broadly speaking, traditional ads usually aren't the best choice.

My bachelor's degree thesis, way back in the day, was on personal use of social media and how it correlates to popularity and social status in real life. I don't think it was very groundbreaking at all (my half-assed data set didn't reveal much), but I quickly realized that social media platforms are very, very fleeting.

I've found that a very useful tool to gauge popular perceptions is Google Trends. Simply tracking the volume of searches for particular channels can give you a great idea of the attitude towards different social platforms.

It's not surprising that platforms like Google Plus or Tumblr have seen a steadily declining amount of interest over time. The same happened with Vine, except that for the huge spike in searches when it was announced that it was closing.

LinkedIn stays pretty much the same, with a slight increase, although it sees dips every year around Thanksgiving and Christmas. Facebook and Twitter have been seeing declining rates of interest since 2014. On the other hand, Instagram and Reddit have both increased since then.

What can we learn from these patterns? Many things. First, don't put all your eggs in one basket. And probably most importantly, remember that public opinion changes quickly and carries powerful momentum. Once a MySpace dies, it fades from memory pretty quickly.

WHAT TYPE OF CONTENT WORKS ON SOCIAL MEDIA?

When you're creating content for social media, you're working in an entirely different medium than most advertising or marketing channels. You're operating within the confines of a person's social life, rather than just trying to hit them with a message in public while they're out and about.

You'd think that would be fairly obvious, but so many companies don't take advantage of this. That's why you see so many salesy, hard-hitting ads on Facebook.

(And, by and large, those ads don't work.)

Social media provides a very specific sort of platform in which you get to know users as individuals rather than mass of generic consumers. This is a huge advantage. Of course, social media comes with some huge downsides as well.

Generally, social media users aren't actively looking to be sold something. They don't necessarily expect or want to be advertised to. This is the opposite of what happens with Google search advertising, for example, where ads can be targeted towards someone who is searching for "best new car for families."

Social media works best with two primary goals: impulse purchases and branding. The higher the cost of your product, the less likely someone will convert directly to a sale coming from social media. However, using social media as branding for a multi-channel campaign is always a good idea if the budget allows for it. And gadgets or impulse purchases, especially if they're easy and low-cost, can do well, too.

You can also advertise niche products to niche audiences via social media. For example, promoting sewing machine accessories to people heavily interesting in quilting can yield great results. The content used in this social targeting, however, doesn't need to be salesy. People are swiftly getting tired of being sold something every day, and they don't really need many more things. The content needs to be educational or informative, and establish the brand as an authority within the niche.   With the huge volume of low-quality, churned-out content being farmed on the internet today, extra effort always goes a long way.

WHAT DOES IT TAKE TO STAND OUT ON SOCIAL?

It's still entirely possible to stand out and gain significant traction in social media. But it's extremely difficult, and I'd venture to say extremely rare, to be able to accomplish this—partly because it's only possible via scale. Anyone can spin up an edgy Twitter account and start making jokes, but if you've only got 150 followers, you're not going to see a lot of growth. On the other hand, if you've got 15,000 followers you'll probably see some organic growth. There is an unseen threshold—a sort of inertial mass that must be overcome to push beyond your direct reach.

One of the best examples of a corporate account wildly succeeding is the Wendy's Twitter account.

Amy Brown was the manager of the corporate Wendy's account for over four years. When people asked the Wendy's Twitter account for directions to the nearest McDonalds, she replied with a picture of a trashcan. When another user said "I bet you won't follow me," she replied with "You won that bet."

A constant stream of sarcastic, yet never mean-spirited tweets directed against McDonalds and Burger King paid off, because the strategy went viral.

Here's the deal, though: this only works because of scale. Sassy tweets are only so effective because it's ridiculous and unexpected for a large corporate account. If your local burger joint makes derogatory comments about the taco place down the road, it doesn't quite carry the same heft.

Managing social media on a team can be an exercise in patience—maintaining a constant voice is a problem, since the mediums of Twitter, Facebook, and other platforms are so individual by design.

Vlad Calus is the co-founder of Planable, a social media collaboration software for marketing teams, agencies, and freelancers. Planable is used by more than 5000 brands worldwide, including Jaguar, BMW, and Virgin Mobile. Vlad founded two nonprofits at the age of sixteen, and eventually dropped out of college and built Planable with two friends. The startup has seen considerable success, being funded by Techstars London. In 2018, Vlad became a Forbes 30 Under 30 honoree. As the marketing face of Planable, his day-to-day job involves acquiring new customers and making sure the existing ones stay happy. I first ran into Vlad's business in a coworking space in Moldova, and I've been following his team's progress ever since.

I sat down and, considering the fact that he's a young guy in a tech-focused career, asked him what drove him to create Planable. I also asked him if he had always known he'd be in the business of software.

"I feel like I was the youngest guy everywhere I went," Vlad said, "in projects, nonprofit organizations, companies, and small gigs to earn some peanuts in a post-Soviet country. The funny thing is, I never imagined myself building a tech company. I always dreamed of becoming a pilot at Emirates Airlines. Always in the air, visiting and traveling 100 countries a year, and being a citizen of the world.

"Planable started as an experiment, a playground, and something I wanted to try. Our team met at Startup Weekend Moldova where one of my current co-founders was pitching an idea at the event. When we gathered as a team, we quickly understood we shared the same frustrations. We all worked in agencies and hated sending back-and-forth emails to our clients in spreadsheets and Powerpoints. It was a complete chaos to receive approval on the content or feedback to implement. It all started from our personal need, and then we quickly understood that there are many agencies that share the same frustration as we do. So we wanted to fix that."

"So, your product was created to improve efficiency," I said. "If you could snap your fingers and change one aspect of marketing, what would it be? In other words, how could an entry-level marketer make it better?"

"Marketers have a huge opportunity," he replied, "technology has enabled them to deliver personalized content at the fingertips of their audiences. On the other side, marketing has a content creation bottleneck that's fundamentally limiting the way it works.

"Scaling content marketing is a problem that isn't solved just by throwing more people or tools in the situation. You need to update processes, strategies, and more automation. And that's exactly what we're working on solving.

"When I think about what aspect of marketing should be changed, there are always three things in my mind. I think about clarity, I think about coordination, and I think about efficiency. Clarity with easy access to information. You need to build a workspace that provides clarity to make decisions and to execute effective content. When marketers don't have access to all the information, a lot of time and effort is wasted and sometimes overlapping work is produced. Marketers need to be empowered to see the big picture and understand where their work fits in the puzzle. The ability to clearly visualize past, present, and future content brings to light new opportunities, patterns, or gaps. When marketers have ready access to the information they need to produce work, they deliver better results. Understand the brand, channels, and visual identities. When you work with multiple people, teams, partners and marketing channels, you run the risk of introducing inconsistency and publishing confusing messages. You also need the right content management tool to ensure consistency. You need a tool that helps you label, organize and more importantly visualize the content. When the content is very visual, it's easy to see what stands out and is not on brand.

"Coordination with better feedback and communications to prevent feedback paralysis will dramatically reduce feedback cycles and make it dead simple for your team to work with you. Feedback needs to be in context, and it needs to be in real time. Marketing moves fast, and email just doesn't move at the speed of our industry. We need a way to communicate feedback that is instant, at the speed of thought. We need a way to make approvals fast and clear, no second thought if something has been approved or not. We need to give feedback that is in context, next to the content itself. This communication needs to be where it logically makes sense, in the same space where in the content is.

"And efficiency. We need to get back our nights and weekends in order to stay creative and strategic. There's a lot of space for improving our efficiency as an industry. Adjust your processes. Very often I see marketers trying to solve their problems by implementing technology, when their problems are actually people or process problems. I think it's very important to fix your process problems before buying tech, because you're just going to end up replicating those problems inside the technology."

He's right—none of us know what we're doing. And if anyone says differently, they're probably not very self-aware. I asked him which hard skills he thought were most important for today's fresh college graduate as they embark upon a career in marketing.

"Storytelling is an essential element of marketing. It drives the reader into your content and improves your chances for engagement, conversion, or purchase. Are you able to fit a captivating story in a social media post with 140 characters? That's the question you should find an answer for, if you're just starting your career in digital marketing. Find stories and understand how to spin them in the best possible way using your copywriting skills."

Vlad sees himself as a mentor for students in the future. "I envision myself as a mentor for students and fresh college graduates to help them build a startup that they're really passionate about. I'm obsessed with helping other people. I was joking with my significant other that I want to retire financially by 30 and never work a day more, but the truth is—I can't imagine myself not working and looking for a new adventure. Which means I'll be constantly looking to build new companies, because that's who I am."

ADVERTISING ON SOCIAL

Advertising on social media is like entering someone's living room and trying to sell them something. You're in their territory: social media is such an intensely personal and (sometimes) private platform that you can't use the same strategies as you might in other channels.

Advertising on social platforms tends to work drastically different for each niche, so there's no secret method of doing it right. You'll see varying levels of ad success based upon which category your business occupies. So, when you don't know what to do, testing is the best way to find an answer.

When we started working with one of our clients, the stories they shared from working with a previous agency were so dismal that they didn't even want to try Facebook again. Our client's single thought was "Facebook is just not for us."

We can't really blame him. When we looked at the numbers from the client's previous Facebook ad campaign, it wasn't encouraging. The cost was extremely high, and the campaign simply wasn't profitable.

As we sat down to analyze their previous results, we saw that out of the $1190 he spent, only 28 of the 4,295 total clicks came from desktop; the only 2 conversions from his entire campaign came from those 28 desktop clicks.

Essentially, he was spending thousands on mobile clicks, which never converted. The $54 he spent on desktop clicks, however, did convert! He spent $1,136 on mobile clicks, but these were simply cheap and easy clicks with no conversion. It made the campaign "seem" successful (looking like a lot of people were interested in the ad), but in reality, it wasn't worth his money at all.

One reason it wasn't converting was that the client's web app (used to monetize leads) was not optimized for a mobile experience— so all the ad money spent on mobile views was essentially wasted. Also, the campaign had used "audience network" views, ads that appear within mobile apps and mobile websites. Usually, those are pop-ups, which firstly, annoy everyone, and secondly, can be easily clicked accidentally by users. These audience network ads spent 73% of the budget. This made the real cost per engagement look small, and showed a huge click-through rate with no real results.

What did we do to fix it? Here's where the testing comes in. We started with excluding any mobile traffic, focusing on desktop (the Facebook newsfeed only). We wanted to test results between some classic ads and boosting a blog post, so we set up an A/B test. The results were impressive: within a couple weeks, the client had already gained 9 conversions for far less money than they'd spent on the previous 2 conversions.

That's when we realized that people don't react to classic Facebook ads anymore. Users have developed a sort of allergy to them. Our research showed that a higher relevance score means a lower price. Relevance score is an estimate of how many people click on an ad (CTR), how many people interact with your ad (post likes, comments, shares), and their landing page experience.

Also, we found some interesting info regarding posts:

✦ Using the same targeting, posts (informational articles, to be specific) perform better than ads.

✦ Posts inherently have a better relevance score.

✦ People engage more with a post than with an ad; it provides more value than an ad.

✦ People share posts a lot—this means more people are seeing it for free (people don't share ads).

✦ Posts with the right question increase organic traffic. People seeing a "how much does this cost" post search it on Google, where they find the client from PPC ads or organic ranking. This builds trust and additional organic traffic.

Knowing this information, we stopped making classic ads for this client. We tested different articles, carefully watching how people reacted to each. The targeting we ultimately decided to use was mostly retargeting and lookalike campaigns, which build a similar audience based on your existing customers and website visitors.

CONTENT FOR SOCIAL PLATFORMS

You want content that engages readers, and ultimately, brings conversions. For people to engage with content, it must have an intrinsic value. It has to inform, educate, solve problems, or entertain. It can be a post, an image, or a video. The main idea is that it should not look like an ad (never like you want to sell them something); instead, you should ask an opinion, talk to the audience, and answer their questions. Tell them how you can help them and what makes you different from the others.

Good content can ask for an opinion (so the customer feels important), like: "If you would do X, how would you do it?" or "What stops you from doing X?" or "What scares you about X?" or "How do you think X can change your life?" or "If you could only have 5 things to take with you for X, what would they be?" It can also provide valuable answers to questions that matter to the customer, like: "How to save money on X" or "How to do X with $1,000." Your product can be an answer for other questions. Like "10 Vacation Alternatives You Should Consider," or "19 Things You Could Buy Instead of a College Education." If your product is expensive or oriented to the luxury market, frame it as an alternative for something that is also expensive, not be the alternative for something inexpensive. If it's an app that's being sold for $1.99, frame it as an alternative for something inexpensive, like a candy bar or a coffee.

The field of social media changes fast—platforms fall in and out of favor with the general public, and it seems like new unicorns rise to the surface every few months. What's important is remembering that in the end all platforms are similar—it's the theory behind social media that remains, in most cases, the same. You're approaching people on their home turf, so to speak—and you've got to remember to treat them as if they're in their own home. Pushy sales rarely work; it's more about branding and building a faithful audience.

EMAIL MARKETING

"Simplicity is the keynote of all true elegance."
- Coco Chanel

Email marketing isn't sexy, but ignoring it in your marketing strategy is a colossal mistake. In this chapter, we'll cover some email basics, and why it's so important to utilize this channel in your strategy.

Sometime in late 1971, a researcher at DARPA named Ray Tomlinson sent the first network email through ARPANET. It was just a test message to himself. He can't remember what it said, but he thinks it was something like, "QWERTYUIOP."

Not long after, the first commercial email message was sent on May 3rd, 1978 by Gary Thuerk. He sent an email promoting DEC computers to a list of 400 recipients. Since ARPANET was a government-sponsored network, he faced severe reprisals. However, the single spam email resulted in over $13 million in sales.

I doubt any spam email has since eclipsed that incredible number. However, email marketing is still one of the most profitable channels in digital marketing, and it's also one of the most overlooked—you won't see a lot of fanfare about it.

See, digital marketers have a tendency to go towards the flashy new things. We're sort of like developers, who see a fancy new technology and decide it's essential to implement in every single one of their projects.

Of course, we can easily see the fallacy when it's in a different industry! You don't need to build a self-healing, load-balancing Kubernetes cluster, when WordPress works just fine for a personal blog. So why do we need to try Snapchat sponsored posts, when an email campaign is simpler, cheaper, and 100% proven?

Although it's always good to try new ideas, don't abandon the tried and true. It may not be glamorous, but email marketing consistently provides one of the highest returns on investment of any digital marketing channel in existence.

BUILDING AN EMAIL LIST

Everyone hates spam. And everyone equally hates highly promotional emails. That's why overly salesy campaigns won't find much success: the key to a good email marketing campaign is building a brand and building an audience, not specifically selling something right away.

Building an email list is not easy. You can't buy a quality list, and there really aren't any shortcuts. You just have to slowly build up a list over time—there are a few ways to do this. One of the best and most sustainable ways is by creating quality content and offers that compel your customers to come back for more.

Over the years a lot of tools and techniques have popped up for "hacking" your email list growth, but ultimately they only increase your signup rates—they don't create them. If you only have 10 signups a month, improving your signup rates by 10% doesn't do a whole lot—you won't get a whole lot of pizzazz from that single extra signup. Adding toolbars and large buttons and forms won't bring people to your site; you have to create something worth visiting. There's a lot of content out there—and a lot of it is good content. So, you're going to have to differentiate yourself by making great content. Unfortunately for you, there's also a whole lot of great content out there.

So what are some of the sources for your email list? First off, your personal contacts and network are a great start. Chances are, you've got a few hundred folks you know personally from work, school, or everyday life. Now, emailing them is a huge relational risk —it's not something to do lightly. If you're an annoying sort of person, just don't do this. But if you think you're likable—well, maybe a gentle, personal email isn't the worst way to get your first few subscribers. If you've got friends you think might be interested, send them an email and say you're starting a newsletter, and if they want in, tell them to shoot you an email so you can add them.

Another source of potential email leads are your social media contacts. You probably have more contacts on your various social media platforms than you may know in real life, so try posting to your social media and asking if anyone would be interested in your newsletter. Here's an easy hack: if you're active on LinkedIn, simply visit every one of your contact's profiles and grab their email address. Then send a mass email out, asking if they'd like to opt-in to your newsletter.

Just these few tactics should give the average person a couple hundred subscribers, a nice jumpstart to your list; but you also want strangers, right? If you could make money only by selling to your friends, you'd be lucky indeed. So make sure your website has an easy way for visitors to sign up to your list. A certain percentage of visitors, whether from organic or paid sources, will sign up—it's a slow but sure way to build your list.

We practice a very low-visibility, non-annoying approach to email capture. It's less efficient than an annoying email splash page, but we don't believe in gatekeeping, and we know that being too aggressive would damage our brand.

ENGAGING YOUR LIST

So ultimately, you've got an email list because you want to make more money. But if you use your email marketing strategy as a way to drive sales primarily, rather than brand, you're going to be in for a rough surprise.

Think about your inbox. How many emails do you get each day? How many of those do you actually want to open and read? How many actually give you a little bit of enjoyment, satisfaction, education, or value? Very few. The vast majority can be written off immediately—I get about a hundred emails a day offering SEO services, mail-order Viagra, princely sums of money, testosterone shots, and trips to Cancun. Even on the educational end of the spectrum, it's either a string of gurus offering expensive courses on self-improvement, or a financial advisor peddling insurance or investments.

Email recipients have been bombarded with pushy sales emails for thirty years now. We're now all fairly savvy, but that doesn't mean tactics don't still work. Unfortunately, many marketers are predatory, and this is a shame (usually trying to sell someone's grandmother a timeshare or the secret to everlasting youth). But the actual secret is: the best marketers aren't predatory—they're just creative.

Email campaigns are branding. They are one of the most affordable, efficient, lasting, and flexible ways to build an incredibly engaged audience. If you've got the ideas, skills, and persona, a simple newsletter can be one of the most powerful weapons in your arsenal.

On the other hand, a poorly executed email campaign can be a bomb that goes off in your lap, destroying all the trust you've worked so hard to build over the years.

The key is understanding your audience. If you're lucky enough to have an audience that looks forward to being bombarded with 7 emails a week, surge forward! But if your audience is realistic, well, be careful you don't alienate them with countless pitches. Nothing kills a campaign quicker than a dozen spam reports, bad online reviews, and fiery email complaints.

Although email has been abused by countless spammers, scammers, and even many well-meaning but naive marketers, there have always been some excellent newsletters written by both individuals and companies, and you should model yours after these. Some of the most successful are highly informational, industry-specific newsletters catering to a narrow but involved cadre of recipients. Others are personal and usually entertaining email updates that feel relatable—sort of the original blogger. Companies have used emails to make their audience feel like part of a family, and even if they don't directly push a product, brand loyalty increases, and ultimately, sales increase as well.

The difficulty is that many marketers are working with small, mom-and-pop style businesses. And if you don't have an audience, or just a small audience, there's not a lot of bandwidth to design a long-term branding strategy, cross your fingers, pull out the checkbook, and hope for the best.

That doesn't mean there's no room for email marketing at all. For local businesses, offering unique discounts for signing up to the list can incentivize brick-and-mortar customers, and even pull in foot traffic when needed. Often, when the people who sign up to your list are actual people who've actually been on your premises, they're much more favorable to getting offers in their inboxes. Not so much if you're a random SaaS company offering 5% off today for ordering some fancy new CRM software.

Keep Email Design Simple

Tools like MailChimp, ConstantContact, or Aweber make it extremely easy to manage lists, send emails, and design attractive emails. However, there's a catch-22: the more people use such tools, the less a good design sets you apart.

Even if you've never opened MailChimp in your life, head over to your inbox and open ten promotional emails you last received. Chances are, you will recognize the standard MailChimp template in at least two or three.

It's not bad—but it's not good either. Even though you can embed images, video, polls, all sorts of things within your emails, it doesn't mean you should. Sometimes, the writing is what matters. We've seen results come from simple emails containing only text that were better than the fanciest, embed-heavy emails that were basically entire inbox microsites. So, focus on your reader. What would you want if you were them? A fancy header and an image-littered email that takes a while to download, or just a simple, to-the-point message?

SEGMENTATION

For a while now, segmentation has been a fancy word within the email marketing world. Basically, segmentation means separating parts of your audience into groups and sending different messages to each one.

There's nothing inherently wrong with this approach, and it works great on a macro level. For example, you wouldn't want to send retirement advice to all of the college kids on your list, just like you wouldn't want to send a "Top 10 Spring Break Spots" email to a bunch of old folks.

It's important to be wary of overly segmenting, because if your business is thriving and self-aware, chances are you know who you need to be targeting. And if you know who you want to target, chances are that with a little extra effort, you can craft a message that resonates with your entire audience; some things truly resonate with everyone, whether they're 22 or 82.

One use of segmentation is sending different messages to people who've gone through different phases of their relationship with your company. For example, sending specific emails to people who added an item to their cart but didn't check out. Or sending special offer emails to your regular returning customers who've bought from you a dozen times. Or sending emails to people who've never bought from you. This is very useful, and can usually be configured within your email program and e-commerce platform quite easily.

It's still important to remember that people are real people. Don't treat them like a statistic within your database. Be very careful about your messaging, because people realize more and more that every company they've ever interacted with holds precious data on their purchasing habits. Be conscious of your user's privacy, and they'll respect that.

BUYING EMAIL LISTS

From time to time, you might see someone recommend buying an email list, or renting an email list. We have a quite simple answer for this: don't. For one thing, depending upon your jurisdiction, buying an email list might not be entirely legal. And for another thing, blindsiding people with cold emails is a pretty iffy tactic, unless you're a Nigerian prince, and then it somehow seems to work.

Unless you've got a very close partnership with a company whose audience is aligned with yours, borrowing a list is a very expensive and inefficient way of marketing. It's slower, but we recommend building your own. It almost always offers better results and can become a valuable asset. In the right hands, your email list can be a major part of your company's revenue simply through good branding and strategy.

CASE STUDY: REVIVING AN OLD EMAIL LIST

Several years ago, we worked with a client who had a large email list (of around 20,000 past customers) but hadn't been actively using their list. In an effort to improve branding and possibly gain some sales, we decided to try to revive this list.

We started off by sending a "cleanup" message. This was essentially a polite, short email notifying everyone on the list that we were about to email them a regular newsletter, and encouraging them to unsubscribe if they didn't want to receive the emails.

This may seem counter-intuitive, but it's actually not. You want to be talking to people who open, read, and enjoy your emails —not those who get frustrated and mark it as spam.

We got a few unsubscribes, and a few bounces from emails that weren't even in existence anymore. Then, we started sending a weekly email. It wasn't salesy; we didn't push any products or services. We just wrote a short, simple email each week with a couple of links to helpful how-to articles on the website. We just wanted to remind users that the company existed!

We also focused on writing funny, natural-English email headlines in order to differentiate us from all the spam that inboxes usually find themselves cluttered with.

The company told us that a good goal for the open rate (which is typically how you measure email campaign success) was around 8%, and their former campaign had usually met that goal.

After four or five weeks, our new email campaign was averaging over 15% open rate, and sometimes over 20%.

WEB DEVELOPMENT

"Never trust a computer you can't throw out a window."
- Steve Wozniak

Imagine having incredible marketing strategies, huge budgets, and multiple channels at your disposal, but no way to implement. Without solid web development knowledge, it's like having lots of nails with no hammer. Today's marketer absolutely has to know their way around HTML, WordPress, and basic scripting. To the uninitiated, it sounds like a lot, but it's one of the most important things you can learn.

Today's most successful digital marketer is a hybrid between a developer and a traditional marketer.

For many years, the two worlds were exclusive. Marketing and development were two different departments on either side of the moon, and communications between the two were confusing at best, antagonistic at worst. The friction was palpable (and still is, at a lot of companies). On one hand, the marketers were convinced that they're the only reason the company has any business, and that the developers are just some expensive code monkeys (it's kind of true). On the other side, the developers are convinced they're the only reason the company works, and that the marketers are just some impractical salespeople (it's kind of true).

But the new reality is that the two worlds are now one. If you've got marketing with no tech skills, you've got nothing to give anyone. And if you've got tech skills with no marketing, guess what? You've just built a product with no users.

New marketers can not only interface with development in an intelligent way, but actually implement and play a heavy part in the development process themselves. This requires some give and take between the two worlds.

Not only have many individual hybrid roles in marketing and development been created recently, but in many cases, the lines have been blurred until there's no difference between the two. Often a front-end developer sits on the intersection: someone who understands branding and communication, but who can also hook up an API and spin up servers.

Now, a tech-heavy career might not be everyone's cup of tea, and there are definitely still roles for marketers that don't require any significant tech skills. But those roles are going the way of the dodo. If you want to be relevant five or ten years from now, you need to know your way around web development.

In the past few years, many self-hosted website platforms have popped to the surface—Wix, SquareSpace, Weebly, and a few other weird names. On one hand, this is an incredible benefit, because the barrier to entry to getting up and running with a website is very low —if you can follow the steps in a simple wizard, you, too, can have a website. On the other hand, I've seen that most freshly graduated marketers use these platforms for their own personal sites. And while that's fine—it's not fine. None of your clients are going to be using these platforms, for multiple reasons. They're not customizable, they're not optimized, they cost on a monthly basis, and they're very difficult to extend. So, if you want to help clients who are running real sites on their own servers, you've got to learn how to work with the actual internet.

If you're a digital marketer, there are some basic hard skills you'll need in order to stay relevant in the field. These are:

+ A solid understanding of HTML
+ Ability to edit existing CSS frameworks
+ Ability to edit existing CSS frameworks
+ Ability to install and edit WordPress sites
+ Ability to implement e-commerce sites
+ Basic ability to use analytics and tracking plugins and parameters
+ Ability to use FTP
+ Ability to set up hosting, register domains, and configure DNS settings

These are the bare minimums needed. If you don't know how to do all of these, you will have to figure it out at some point in your marketing life. There are additional hard skills that might not be absolutely necessary, but will be extremely useful in your career. They're skills that might only need to be used a few times, but being adept at these will greatly increase your value in the field. These are: a solid knowledge of PHP, a basic understanding of web-focused languages like Python or Ruby, and perhaps some tidbits of how to administrate an Apache server.

Learning Basic HTML & CSS

If you grew up as a kid in the era of MySpace and forums, you probably know a bit of HTML and don't even realize it.

You don't have to know how to build a website from scratch, although that level of skill will definitely help your career. You really just need to know the basics of how a website works on the internet and how to edit it.

The first thing to understand is that HTML (hyper text markup language) and CSS (cascading style sheets) aren't really programming, they're scripting. HTML simply tells the browser how to display the content within the file, and the CSS makes it pretty. It doesn't need to be compiled or otherwise prepped, just opened with a browser.

Knowing the basics of how a website is displayed will help vastly in a marketing career, even if it's not your main focus. You'll be working with countless development teams, webmasters, bloggers, e-commerce sites, and designers, and knowing what they're doing on the back end will make you a well-rounded player on the team.

You can easily build a site with a few pages of HTML and CSS. A huge number of open-source templates and frameworks are available online, and these are customizable with just a few lines of code. It's worth experimenting in order to see how far you can take your editing skills.

Hosting, Domains, and FTP

So, you've got a site on your computer. Congratulations! Now the world needs to see it.

If code intimidates you - study it! It's easier than you think.

Your website begins its life in a folder on your computer. Only you and your browser can see it. You've got to put it on a server so everyone out there has access to it, too.

So, you get hosting. The level of hosting you get depends on your needs, but most small businesses just need an average shared hosting package that costs $10-20 per month (you can host many different sites on one server). If you're selling items, it's probably worth going with an e-commerce platform like Shopify, unless you've got the development chops to implement WooCommerce or a similar standalone e-commerce platform.

Then, you register a domain. You point the domain at your hosting server using DNS configuration. Then, you upload your site files to the server. Usually, you can do this via FTP or shell access. Download a FTP manager like FileZilla or CyberDuck which helps you do this within a graphical interface.

At this point, you've got your own website. You own this site and control it, and can put anything on it that you want. Go crazy!

CONTENT MANAGEMENT SYSTEMS

I developed my first Wordpress website in 2006, after a couple years of looking for a solid content management system.

In those days, there weren't a whole lot of options for a good CMS. It was either develop your own site from scratch (something I ended up doing for the majority of static sites those days), or use a content management system like Movable Type, Wordpress, or Joomla (can anyone say *ugh!*)

Even Wordpress was only best of the worst. It was huge, clunky, buggy, insecure, and a pain to customize. Since then, I've worked on dozens, if not hundreds of Wordpress installations, fittingly so, since an estimated 27.5% of the known sites on the internet use Wordpress as a framework.

And Wordpress is *still* only best of the worst. It is still huge, clunky, buggy, insecure, and a pain to customize. Why, then, do a third of websites use this outdated, clunky, neolithic tool?

In part, because it's highly extensible, almost everyone knows how to work with it, it's got a huge community for support, and it works on any server running PHP and MySQL. It's also almost impossible to migrate away from.

Migrating WordPress—either to another WordPress site or to an entirely different content management system—is one of the most agonizing processes I've ever had to go through, and this includes my Windows XP days where I was reinstalling from the CD every few months. It's not automated. It has never proceeded without errors or incompatibilities. And I think in every single case, I've had to go into the SQL database and manually change field values.

In the world of amazingly streamlined frameworks with file sizes of a couple MB, flat file systems like MySQLite, and bulletproof cloud hosting, why are we still using Wordpress?

There are a few answers.

As I mentioned before, everyone else is using it. And this is a legitimate reason, even if it's fundamentally flawed. When consensus develops, so does support, documentation, plugins, and in the case of Wordpress, an entire cottage industry of developers.

Another reason is lack of creativity. There are literally hundreds of alternatives to Wordpress. There are artfully coded static HTML templates out there, like Bootstrap, Skeleton, Boilerplate, *ad nauseum*. There are sophisticated app frameworks, like Django. And there are infinitely better e-commerce platforms out there, like Shopify or Magento.

Another? Fear of the unknown. Why try something else when all I've been using for the past decade is this?

And finally, it does work for a lot of applications. And it does a lot of things pretty solidly. Wordpress isn't always the devil: it actually works quite well when you have a great deal of content to manage. For content-focused brands, or newspapers, or large blogs, it does serve its purpose well.

What are some better alternatives?

First, for smaller "brochure sites," the sort of website a small business needs for online exposure, there is little reason to use a content management system. Hundreds of quality HTML5+CSS3 templates exist, with some of the highest quality available for free commercial use.

Second, for smaller dynamic sites without custom functionality (this could include any "brochure-type" site which does need regular updating), there are a few really solid, lightweight CMS platforms. Ghost is one of the highest-rated. Jekyll is another acclaimed system. For complex sites with a lot of functionality required, Django is an amazing Python-based web app framework which is lightweight, easily extensible, and uses a MVC model for advanced development —but you're not going to set this one up unless you're a full-fledged developer.

For e-commerce websites, one positive trend we've seen in the industry is a proliferation of e-commerce as a service—with players like Shopify and BigCommerce making it extremely easy and affordable to spin up a web shop. The WordPress equivalent, WooCommerce, isn't half as easy, affordable, dependable, or reliable as Shopify.

However, with all that complaining out of the way, WordPress is still the mothership of content on the internet, and it's absolutely crucial that even new marketers know their way around the system.

In summary, web development is an essential part of marketing. It's the hammer with which you secure all the individual nails. You don't have to be a programming expert to be a good marketer. But you absolutely have to know *something* about how the internet works, otherwise you'll be swimming upstream. The ability to register a domain, get hosting, edit a website, publish a website, know your way around WordPress, and use FTP are some of the bare essentials for today's marketer.

BRANDING, MESSAGING, & WRITING

"The most important thing is to read as much as you can, like I did. It will give you an understanding of what makes good writing and it will enlarge your vocabulary." - J. K. Rowling

Tone of voice is very important—we all know this. Often, the tone of a discussion can mean a lot more than the actual words being said. This is also the case in marketing. You can say all the right things, but if the vibe feels wrong, nobody will trust your brand. Ad copy, calls-to-action, product descriptions—all will be much more effective if you learn how to create the right tone.

One of the most important things to understand about creating a profitable campaign is that success doesn't depend on the campaign alone. There are a lot of factors in play; one of the most crucial factors is knowing how to convert visitors once they visit your site. You can have the best ad campaign in the world, but if your site sucks, you won't make any profit.

We'll take a brief look at various aspects of your website which need to be addressed in order to see great results from any marketing campaign: your company's branding, your messaging and tone of voice, and your copywriting.

If you've spent any amount of time in the digital marketing world, you've probably heard about terms like "banner blindness" or "advertising blindness." But what does it actually mean, and how can we fight it? I have to confess that I create online ads for a living—and I also use an ad blocker. Who wouldn't? One of the benefits of using an ad blocker is that you can see the exact number of ads that have been blocked on each page.

Guess how many ads you see while watching a YouTube video? Maybe five or ten? No, right now Opera is telling me it's blocked 55 ads on just one video. We see thousands of ads per day. Long ago we started, consciously or not, trying to ignore web advertising.

Ad blindness is the phenomenon of users ignoring every ad they see, or anything that even looks like an ad. Ad blindness on the internet developed along with the rise of ads themselves. The more you see, the more you ignore.

It doesn't mean that, as advertisers, we don't have a chance. We still have the possibility of gaining visibility. We just need to understand that as the internet evolves, customers evolve, too. So should our ads. After all, no one likes being told what to do, and we most certainly don't want 55 different companies telling us what to do.

The first thing to remember is that salesy ads don't work anymore. Users want to be educated, entertained, and informed. Or, they just want to feel something (happiness, sadness, nostalgia, etc). Whether it's a video, display ad, or even just a search ad, today's audiences want to be given a chance to choose the product by its benefits, and not just succumb to whichever ad writes "buy now" or "click here" with the biggest font.

AD WRITING & MESSAGING

Writing ads is a mixture of science and art. It's a combination of a hard skill and a soft skill. It's one of those things things that's useless without an intuitive understanding of human behavior and the psychology behind what drives people. But, it's equally useless without organized testing and optimization.

In preparation for a conference talk in London, Anya decided to present about banner blindness: why people ignore ads, and how to avoid it during the creation of your own ads. The November before the talk, we ran a survey on current perceptions of advertising. In preparation for Anya's presentation, we decided we needed to gather data and gain insight into the current popular perceptions of advertising. We kept the survey short and simple, but I think we gained some valuable info from it.

We asked a range of questions, from which types of ads are the most annoying to what sort of ads offend most. We also collected the standard pack of demographic-related materials in order to determine the education, age, and technical proclivity of our audience. I'll go through our results, then unpack it a little bit with our theories and observations!

We wanted to know which sorts of ads are most annoying and least annoying. Respondents had to pick three out of seven ad types as most annoying, and had to do the same for least annoying. We listed these ad types for them to select: full-page magazine ads, billboards on the highway, Google search text ads, product ads on

Instagram, banner ads on websites, 30-second TV commercials, radio advertisements, and Video ads that play before a YouTube video.

The most hated forms of ads? In order from most annoying to least:

1. YouTube ads
2. Radio ads
3. 30-second TV spot
4. Banner ads in websites
5. Text ads on Google SERPs
6. Instagram product ads
7. Billboards on the highway
8. Full-page magazine ads

We also wanted to know how many people used an ad blocker plugin. Responses were evenly distributed: 49.3% of respondents indicated they use an ad blocker plugin. 50.7% don't.

We also were curious if many people were offended by ads. Responses were also fairly evenly distributed. A slight majority of 52.2% said that they'd never been offended by an ad. 47.8% said they had been offended.

And then, because we were curious how aware people are of the ads that surround them, we asked how many ads per day they thought they were exposed to. As expected, the range here was incredibly wide, but people do know that they see a lot of ads. The peak of the bell curve for respondents? It seems to be that they only notice 100 ads a day.

What sort of ads did people love and hate? We got a wide range of responses for most loved ads, but almost always the ads were humorous, clever, or unique. And they were almost all (around 80%) video ads. Other respondents suggested relevant ads that were well targeted and magazine ads with great photography. Hated ads also got a wide range of responses. The most hated ads were for lingerie brands, political candidates, or pharmaceuticals.

And then, to measure ad effectiveness, we asked if respondents had been introduced to a company or bought a product from an ad in the past 3 months. Over half (52.2%) indicated that an ad had indeed introduced them to a new company or resulted in buying a product in the past 3 months.

Our sample skewed towards younger professionals:

+ 64.2% of respondents indicated they were aged 25-39
+ 20.1% indicated they were aged 40-54
+ 10.4% indicated they were from 55-69
+ And only 4.5% indicated they were aged 18-24

And as far as education,

+ 52.2% of respondents indicated they graduated college
+ 38.8% indicated they had at least a master's degree
+ 9% indicated they had finished high school

Finally, 67.2% of people said they worked in a marketing, advertising, or tech-related field. We thought this was important to ask since the more familiar you are with the way the digital world works, the more biased your answers may be. Our respondents are located globally, with a strong focus in the US. Over 80% are college educated. Around 65% were aged 24-39, while most of the rest were aged 40-54. Around 55% considered themselves savvy in the fields of tech, marketing, or advertising.

As we all know, numbers are finicky things. You can unpack statistics in nearly infinite ways, and your biases will always show up

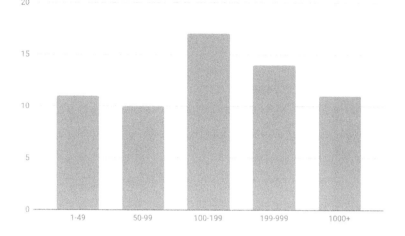

Most respondents thought they saw around 100 ads per day.

in your analysis. These are just our personal reactions to our survey results. So like everything, take them with a grain of salt!

We see more ads than we think. The actual number of ads to which an American is exposed daily is closer to 4000, according to a few studies, so this suggests that we simply don't notice most of the ads we see. Banner blindness!

People don't like being interrupted. It's interesting to note that the most-loved forms of advertising (magazine ads, billboards, and Google search text ads) are also the least time-intrusive ads. They might be prominent in your vicinity, but are easily ignored or dismissed.

The most hated forms of advertising, on the other hand, are YouTube pre-roll ads, TV commercials, and radio commercials. These sorts of ads are extremely intrusive and are time-related rather than space-related; they interrupt your time instead of just the environment around you. However, it's worth considering the secondary effect of this: if people love your ad because it's non-intrusive, are they even noticing it? Or, if it's too intrusive and they do notice it, will it turn them off so much that they never buy from you?

Video ads are polarizing. A cursory glance might indicate that you need to avoid the most-hated forms of advertising—but we don't think that's entirely correct. It's clear that people either love or hate video ads. When we asked people for examples of their favorite specific ads, the responses overwhelmingly indicated people love video ads. At the same time, the specific ads people hated the most were video ads: either on YouTube or TV.

I think this indicates that video ads are polarizing, and whether people like them or not, they tend to grab attention. Unfortunately for advertisers, it's difficult and expensive to produce a good video branding campaign, and it will almost always be reserved for a large company rather than a small business.

Distribution, of course, is another beast. Traditional television programming is prohibitively expensive for most small to medium businesses, but the internet has created a new opportunity in the form of YouTube pre-roll ads, for which you pay per view (usually from $0.01 to $0.10 per view, at least in the United States).

Because videos are so polarizing, however, a video needs to be done right, or you risk alienating a potential user base with annoying, bad quality, or poorly targeted video advertising.

People care about morals. Worth taking a closer look at is the specific content that people tagged as offensive. Less than half of respondents indicated that an ad had offended them, but the reasons given by those who had been offended were almost unanimously for one reason: morals. Respondents listed opposing viewpoints, indecency, or dishonesty as the primary reasons they were offended by an ad. Specifically, respondents indicated that political ads, lingerie ads, and pharmaceutical ads were most offensive to them. Victoria's Secret television ads were called out by a surprisingly large number of respondents as sexist, inappropriate, and embarrassing. I'm very sure that Victoria's Secret knows this and doesn't care. Shock and sex still seems to sell, unfortunately, but unless you're in some sort of lingerie, pharmaceutical, or politics-related industry, you probably don't have to worry too much about upsetting most folks.

People know they're bombarded daily with advertising. They can remember particular ads which made the strongest emotional bond with them, whether through humor, relevance, or endearment. They can also remember particular ads which offended them. They also appreciate non-intrusive, relevant ads—it seems like people have a lot more patience for advertising that takes up their space, rather than their time. After all, what is more precious than time? It's a very finite resource and, as for advertisers, it's probably worth respecting our audience's time.

Include your main features and benefits. What makes you better than your competitor? Do you have anything unique that you provide? What problems does your service or product help solve? What does your customer gain by choosing you?

Add a call to action (CTA). What is the final action you want your users to take when they land on your website? For our example company, we'll choose something like "Get 100% Organic Juice" or maybe "Detox Your Body with Cold Pressed Juices." The last one is both a benefit and a CTA. You want to be smart about your message, as you're limited by the number of characters you are allowed to use.

Avoid repetition! Sometimes, when you don't have any inspiration (or if your products don't really have that many special benefits), it might be hard to come up with great copy. We often see ads that say the same thing in the title, description, and extensions. I'm telling you straight up—it looks bad! You're already limited by the number of characters at your disposal, so don't waste this space. If you have a special offer, use it in the ad! It could be "Free Shipping" or "10% Off Your First Order." Let people know before they even go to your website.

Don't forget to A/B test. There is no single ad structure that works the best for everyone. You have to keep testing different ads and see how they perform. All ad groups should have at least 2-3 ads with slightly different messaging. Once you get around 100 clicks, determine which one has a better CTR (click-through-rate). Look at conversion rates. Which ad gave you more leads? There are ads that have a very high CTR, but users aren't necessarily the same quality as the users of another with lower CTR.

LANDING PAGES

A landing page, also known as a destination page, is the page through which the user enters your website—simple as that. You can even see all of your landing pages, along with their metrics, within Google Analytics.

It's an important part of your campaign, because it's the second thing the user sees, right after he clicks on the ad. The user will generally decide if he trusts you within the first two seconds he lands on the page. The initial first impression will determine in his mind if you're professional and whether he's ready to work with you and buy your services or products.

The landing page experience is part of Quality Score (for channels like Google Ads). This means that the higher the score is, the lower your CPC (cost-per-click) will be. A good landing page experience is directly related to how useful and relevant the user finds the page (some of the metrics that show this relationship are bounce rate and average session duration).

At Discosloth, we run digital ad campaigns. But, we don't only run ads for our clients; we focus just as much on increasing conversions as driving traffic to websites. The most effective ad campaign in the world doesn't matter, after all, if the user has a terrible first impression and experience on your site. Improving your conversion optimization takes the traffic we initially send to the site, and turns those visitors into paying customers.

We've been asked to create landing page solutions for clients. Sometimes, since services exist to autogenerate hundreds of pages based upon keyword lists, clients have the expectation that more is better. Although the answer is different for every situation, in our experience, quality is much better than quantity. That's why we like to emphasize the importance of high quality, carefully researched website content that improves a user's experience, rather than filler content which wastes a user's time.

Why do we care about landing pages so much? Not only do they increase user experience, but a well-designed landing page can boost your Google Ads quality score, which in turn lowers your CPC and increases your ad campaign's return on investment.

A landing page, at it's simplest, is a page that a user lands on after searching for a particular keyword. Landing pages, described abstractly about their most original form, were just detailed pages containing the most pertinent information about a specific product or service. With the advent of inbound marketing and services like HubSpot or InstaPages or Unbounce, however, landing pages began to be commoditized into auto-generated, keyword-stuffed funnel elements.

It's so easy to create a landing page, but it's so hard to create a good one. There are a few reasons why they can be valuable if used appropriately.

1. Your landing page experience is one of the most important factors in decreasing your cost per click in a Google Ads campaign, and most other PPC channels. Google wants to be sure that the search terms users are typing, and the text ads they see, have the same message as the website. But some people use strategies that exaggerate this concept and create a landing page per keyword. This is an over-optimization that Google doesn't appreciate.

2. Landing pages can be essential for A/B testing, giving you a means to experiment with various messaging, design, UX (user experience), and UI (user interface) choices. By default, landing pages are disposable and quickly replaceable, and are therefore perfect for short term testing.

3. If you sell multiple products or services, landing pages can help provide you with simplicity by not showing your user too many options. You can be more relevant to a user's search by having a page with the exact product you're advertising.

But let's back up a bit. Why refer to landing pages as a necessary evil? What's wrong with them? Why did marketers start to abuse them?

Landing pages are an evolutionary byproduct, left over from the prehistoric concept of inbound marketing. Perhaps that's a little harsh, but the internet era of funnels and deceptive psychological tricks is already over: not only are users catching up with the practice, but search engines and ad networks are also penalizing poor design practices.

Essentially, anything that isn't beneficial and constructive for the end user is a net negative for your website's ultimate ranking, conversion, and success. And the search engines know that. That's why landing pages are to be carefully dealt with: tread lightly!

One of the most common myths, usually perpetuated by inbound marketing companies and landing page generators, is that you need to have a separate page for each targeted keyword in order to get high engagement and sales. Some people even tell you to create new websites with new domains. This is an outdated strategy and won't help your sales. Why? Because Google calls these *doorway pages* and they are against Google's policies.

In the world of inbound marketing, a landing page is created for a singular purpose: gaining a conversion. There is usually a simple, clear CTA (call-to-action) which directs users to an action like downloading something or submitting a form. These pages are usually ridiculous. They're not made to add value for users. The only purpose is to create a high-pressure sales environment that encourages the user to BUY NOW, a thousand times. This funnel-loading tactic discourages careful research, and tries to prevent users from leaving to find some other better product. Often, they'll even use mouseover scripts to sense when a user is leaving a page, and then flash a last-minute popup to try to retain a user.

Not all landing pages are evil, of course; the best landing pages are the ones that aren't there to sell, but to create a good experience for users. Google prioritizes pages that provide real value to a user:

either by being educational, entertaining, informative, or useful in some manner.

THREE ELEMENTS OF A GOOD WEBSITE DESIGN

A good website can be boiled down to three factors: first, it converts well. Second, it looks good. Third, it's user-centric.

To convert well, the most important element is the call to action. Every time you add a new CTA on a page, it dilutes the power of the others. It is better to have one call to action than two. It also needs to be above the fold, meaning the user can see it immediately. Other important elements in helping a page convert well are concise messaging (no more than 50 characters for the call to action) and strong visual UI/UX design (a single bold, orange button with a short label). Simplicity and honesty are paramount in creating a site with strong conversion.

Branding must match site-wide. This is important both for credibility and for consistency. It needs to be clutter-free, honest, and simple. If information is extraneous in any way, it doesn't need to be on the landing page. The first page a user visits is the place for total zen minimalism—not for touting the various benefits and features and legal boilerplate of your product. We'll talk a lot more about branding later on.

To be user-centric, it needs to provide value and clarity. Many poorly designed sites and sales strategies are meant to entice or confuse, and this is the worst possible thing that can be done with your page. You have a primary call to action, and whether that CTA is asking for an email address or selling a product, honesty will provide you with only the highest quality users. Make it clear, quick, and effortless for users to interact with your landing page, whether they're on a desktop, iPad, or mobile. It needs to look good, convert well, and be user-centric.

So, what makes a successful site?

- Clear visual design
- Fast load speed
- Mobile-friendly responsive HTML
- Easy-to-read and informative content
- Professional photography
- An easy way of buying or signing up for something

The more you care about good design and good content, the lower your marketing costs will be...and you'll have a higher conversion rate as well.

A consistent user experience throughout the interaction with your brand is important: if the users feel as if they're being bounced back and forth between Facebook, Google Ads, a generated landing page, and your actual website, any trust you've built with them will deteriorate. That's why we so actively discourage the usage of low-cost, high-volume landing page generation services. Not only will this negatively impact your organic rankings, but it decays your brand's identity. It's much better to implement three high quality, carefully researched pages rather than 75 generated pages of churn.

Landing pages are by no means necessary for the success of a PPC campaign (ideally, your website itself will be optimized for conversion well enough already), but when implemented well, landing pages can be an invaluable part of your digital brand.

Branding is a discipline which, ironically enough, suffers from the same vagueness that it seeks to define. People know it's there, they know it's something they're supposed to have, yet more often than not, they have no clue what it is, how to get it, or even why it's important.

Like Justice Stewart famously said during the Ohio obscenity case in 1964: he couldn't define it, but he knows it when he sees it.

And even if we can't define it, we all know a good brand when we see it. We instantly recognize Domino's Pizza, Adidas, Firefox, the Rolling Stones, Porsche, Lego, Levi's, PBR, Hello Kitty, Twitter, and a million others when we see them.

FRIENDLY DESIGN AND INTERFACE

Good design is essential for your website. Good design is not subjective: there are clear factors that go into a good vs. bad design. It's not enough to just use a modern template. A great website requires all aspects of design to work together in a cohesive manner.

Clean, simple layout. Minimalism isn't just a fad. It's an intentional design choice that removes the distractions of a cluttered design in order to emphasize the most important parts. Using appropriate amounts of negative space is not a waste: by isolating the most important elements, you're drawing the eye of the user where the most important content is. Make it simple for the user to understand where they need to click next. Offering a dozen options isn't good: it's better to have one or two buttons.

Consistent branding and color choice. Every part of your website should look like it belongs to your brand. That means using the same font, colors, styling, and design language throughout the entire site. If your company already has an established branding guide, you can use this consistently throughout your site. If not, spend some time developing your *look and feel.* Look and feel is one of the most underrated aspects of a brand. While many are quick to dismiss it as trivial, it's an undeniable part of the success of a website. A website that even looks a couple of years old and has an outdated feel has already lost a level of trust within the first few seconds of the user visiting the page.

Voice and messaging. What attitude does your brand have? Whether it's playful, formal, professional, funny, or sarcastic is up to you. In any case, it needs to be consistent, and this shows in things like your calls to action, page headings, content, colors, and design. For example, if you're a medical consultant, you probably don't want to have a sarcastic tone. You want to convey utmost trust and professionalism, so you pick strong colors like blue and white, you write in clear and formal English, you avoid using too many exclamation points, and choose professional photography. However, if you're a skateboard shop, choosing the formal tone of the medical consultant would be a disaster. You can be irreverent, sarcastic, and edgy. Choose black and red colors, grungy fonts, abstract street photography, and use all the slang you want.

Photography. Professional photography is essential for the most engaging websites. Just using a 24-megapixel camera doesn't make your photography good: make sure that you've got a high level of quality throughout your images. Composition, lighting, clarity, and presentation are of utmost importance.

These steps will go a long way in helping you create a valuable, useful resource that customers will keep coming back to.

CONVERSION OPTIMIZATION

Conversion optimization could have an entire chapter to itself, but it can essentially be boiled down into one simple statement: make it easy.

Everything should be clear and effortless for the customer. Easy to learn about the product, easy to navigate, easy to convert, easy to pay.

Essentially, the more steps you add in between the user first seeing your ad and your final conversion goal, the less likely the user will be to follow through. So keep it simple. Here are some tips to keep in mind:

- Make the call-to-action prominent and clear
- Show plenty of information and images about your product
- Make sure your benefits are clearly shown (free shipping, guarantees, etc)
- Make your conversion goal easy to see (simple, straightforward buttons or forms)
- Offer multiple payment methods (credit cards and PayPal, for example) and an easy checkout process.
- Make sure your site works on all devices
- Make sure your site loads fast

Does site speed affect conversion? The answer: absolutely. Studies have shown that approximately every additional second that a site takes to load can result in up to a 7% reduction in conversions. Numbers vary widely according to your niche and your platform, but you should aim for a page load speed of under 2 seconds.

For example, a few years ago Walmart decided their site wasn't fast enough. They found out that for every 1 second of improvement they experienced up to a 2% increase in conversions. For every 100 milliseconds of improvement, they grew incremental revenue by up to 1%.

IMPORTANCE OF A BRAND

One of the most common assumptions of a company is that you can buy brand. That's only partially true: you can buy half of a brand, but that's just paying for someone to develop the story, the messaging, and the aesthetics. The other half is emotional equity: your brand has to have created and provided enough value that people have been smitten with you. And this can't be bought or faked: it's got to the the reality of the brand.

No matter how much funding is thrown at PR, logo redesigns, ad campaigns, and marketing consultants, if your brand/product/service sucks, then you're just paying for damage control, not progress.

To illustrate this, one of the most hated companies in America, the internet provider Comcast, spent $170 million on marketing in 2012 for their Xfinity Internet brand. In 2015, they spent over $3 billion on advertising. Yet, in 2017, Comcast is still one of the most hated companies in the United States. Consumers only pay for their services because they have a monopoly on internet in many locations. All those billions spent on marketing and advertising and branding have done nothing to erase their image, because they simply provide a horrible experience for their customers.

Then again, there is the opposite story for many companies across the world: there are thousands of companies in all sorts of markets, which offer excellent products and services, yet don't know how to market their brand. No one is aware of their importance, their story, or has any allegiance with their products.

The most visible part of a brand is the look and feel: the logo, colors, layout, and styling of their consumer-facing elements, and the overall aesthetic. When one sees a page on the Apple website, you know it's Apple. They've developed a specific font, color, and style that has been consistent over not only years, but decades.

The most important part about assessing and creating a brand is simply catching up: making sure your website's tech stack isn't built on a 2007 version of Joomla, and making sure your latest social media activity wasn't back in 2015. Creating and maintaining a brand is an ongoing process, and it's easy to fall behind.

But brand aesthetics isn't all that a brand requires. The most important is story: who you are, why you're doing things the way you are, where you're going, and who you want to be. It's also about the users: who uses this product, how does it affect their lives, and why people love the brand.

That's why you can only fake half of branding: you can tell the story, but the rest is up to you by providing the best possible products or services for your audience.

Branding isn't always easy to understand conceptually, but we all know it when we see it. Digital branding includes social media management, advertising, paid campaigns, logo design, conversion optimization, and a host of other tasks with the primary purpose of creating a better user experience.

Once again, it's important to focus on quality rather than quantity. It's becoming harder to game the system, and digital brands are being rewarded more than ever for producing quality shareable content for their audience.

CASE STUDY: HOW BRANDING CAN INCREASE CONVERSIONS

We started branding work on a small private school's digital presence during late 2013, with the goal of a relaunch before the end of the school year. While the reach of the campaign was naturally limited to a small region, the value per acquisition was extremely high (each student attracted would gain the school $7,000/yr for several years). Therefore, the school could justify spending significant resources on improving their branding.

The existing website was built on a Joomla version from 2008 and was comprised of 38 pages. Most of the pages had no more than 3-4 sentences of content. It was almost impossible to navigate, and the blinding blue color theme made it almost painful.

The school had two competitive academies within a 30-mile radius, both of which had much better websites. It was clear which schools had an advantage when prospective parents were researching options.

Although the school didn't want to change logos, we were able to convince them to keep only one of the 3 logos they used in their materials. We totally redesigned the website on a newer, slimmer Wordpress base, spent weeks on shooting new footage and photography, and produced two 30-second commercials and a seven-minute short film.

They were also spending insane amounts of money on radio advertising. We were able to analyze the results and show that the resources spent on radio advertising were too large and was showing a negative return on investment, so we canceled this channel.

Although this rebrand took several months, by the time the school year ended and they opened enrollment for the following semester, they saw a higher number of enrollments by new students than ever before. Due to their enhanced branding and content strategy, this school reached their enrollment cap by the following semester.

Branding and messaging—the tone of a brand's voice—is crucial to developing an effective marketing strategy. Focusing on quality rather than quantity, avoiding cheapened user experiences, and making your messaging friendly rather than pushy, are vital to a campaign's success.

REPORTING, METRICS, & ANALYTICS

*"The key to good decision making is not knowledge. It is understanding.
We are swimming in the former. We are desperately lacking in the latter."*
- Malcolm Gladwell [7]

Marketing often gets a bad rap in the business world. Your colleagues in other departments will claim that it's expensive, it's not easily trackable, and it's usually one of the first expenses to be cut during hard financial times. But digital marketing enables you to track every single dollar spent and determine the return on investment for your company or client. It's one thing to know how your marketing budget is being spent, but knowing how to really use analytics is one of the most important skills in marketing.

Historically, it's true. Marketing has been an extremely non-trackable, mysterious sort of thing. It's never been good at providing proof of itself. Does it work? Did this campaign actually provide X amount of profit?

There's a good reason that marketing has sometimes taken a back seat in company priorities. Sometimes, marketers can be terrible at speaking business language and understanding the importance of profit, margin, cost, and volume; sometimes marketers do a terrible job of marketing ourselves.

Until recently.

See, until the advent of the digital era, the efficacy of marketing campaigns could only be measured with awkward and expensive public perception polls, research panels, estimations, and anecdotal evidence.

Now, we can trace the performance of a campaign all the way from when someone first sees an ad, clicks on an email, puts an item in the shopping cart, and purchases your product. We can nail down the cost per acquisition of a new customer to the exact penny. We can tell that a 54-year-old housewives from New Jersey are 3.2x more likely to order your product than 21-year-old students in Georgia. We can tell that a 35-year-old customer is worth 15% more than a 30-year-old customer. We can know one ad works 25% better than another ad for the same product that uses different wording.

Analytics is one of the most crucial parts of a campaign's performance. If you don't track your results and adjust your campaigns based on data, you're going to waste so much money, it's not even funny. It's a lot to talk about here (we could write a whole book explaining how to measure things), so we'll try to keep it short and to the point.

To make sure you analyze your data correctly, there are a few tools you should use that will help with your data-driven decisions. The main one to start with is Google Analytics.

Google Analytics is a web analytics tool created by Google that allows you to track your website traffic. It's the most commonly used web analytics tool out there, and you can use it for free. Analytics is a very important tool, but underused by the majority of businesses.

Analytics allows you to:

✦ See your website traffic in real time

✦ See audience details like demographics, interests, geo location, and the device and browser they use

✦ Track user engagement, which gives you a grasp of the quality of the traffic you're getting

✦ Analyze your Ads performance per campaign, search queries, destination URLs, and more

✦ Link your search console to Analytics and see data about your organic traffic

✦ Analyze user behavior on your website and see info about site speed, searches that happened on the website, events you are tracking and the performance for each of your pages

✦ See which channels are sending you the best volume of quality traffic

✦ Create your own customized reports, including only the data you need

✦ See all of your conversion data, including which products sold, order value, and other info about user shopping behavior for e-commerce sites

TRAFFIC FROM SOCIAL MEDIA, BING ADS, OR EMAIL CAMPAIGNS

If you are advertising via social media, email marketing, or any other channels where you want to track your campaign separately from organic (unpaid) traffic, make sure you add UTM tracking. UTM tracking is a code added at the end of links that gives Analytics more information about your campaigns. For example, it can tell Analytics that the traffic is coming from a Facebook campaign (looking something like *utm_source=facebook*), from a paid campaign (*utm_medium=cpc*), and that your campaign is about a special promotion you have for organic juice (*utm_campaign=organic_juice_promo*).

A few other tools you should consider:

Hotjar. This is an analytics tool that allows you to record visitors on your website, create heatmaps, and more. It allows you to see first hand what the user is doing on the website, whether they have any struggles finding the info they need, and how they scroll, click, and spend their time.

Google Optimize. This will help you test your website. You can send half of your users to see one variation of your page, and the other half a different one (also known as A/B testing) and see which one has a better performance and higher conversion rate.

Google Ads. Don't forget that Ads has a great Reports section where you can create custom reports and analyze data.

Google Data Studio. This allows you to turn your data into professional reports and house them in dashboards that are easy to read, share and customize.

The internet is full of different tools you can use for your analytics, but the ones above should be your first choice when you are just starting out.

CONVERSION TRACKING

You cannot make data-driven decisions if you cannot associate a conversion (sale, lead, sign-up, etc) with a specific channel or campaign. There are 3 main methods in Google Analytics that help you do this.

Goal tracking. If you have a confirmation page following the user submitting (also known as a *thank-you page*), you can set up a destination goal to track all the users that have reached it.

Event tracking. If you care about form submits, or any other type of button clicks that don't redirect to a thank-you page, you need to set up event tracking. It will allow you to track specific button clicks, video plays, and more.

E-commerce Tracking. If you're an e-commerce website, you might want to track all orders and have the order value shown to you. This implementation requires more code, but the results will be amazing.

WHICH METRICS SHOULD YOU MEASURE?

Once you have Google Analytics set up and your conversion tracking is working, it's time to see how your campaigns are performing. But what should you actually look at to understand if it works? It's hard to have predetermined numbers which you need to see in your website engagement, as it's unique to your niche and type of content.

Analytics does a good job showing you some benchmarking based on your type of business. The main metrics to look at would be: time on page (how long visitors stay on your website), bounce rate (the percentage of single-page sessions in which there was no interaction on the page) and pages/session (average time of pages viewed during a session). Looking at it from a common sense point of view, you want average session duration to be at least a minute, and you want to have a very low bounce rate.

Compare the results between the channels. If your organic traffic has a higher engagement rate, check the search queries. Maybe it's because all organic traffic is coming from brand searches? Analyze the engagement between your pages. Maybe it's one page that brings the average down. See what can be fixed; maybe that page is not highly targeted to your campaigns. If so, A/B test and see if it makes a difference.

If your average time on page is 10 seconds, and your bounce rate is over 90%, something is not working well. Maybe it's not the page, but the traffic you send to it. Check the targeting within your campaign and analyze your search terms. Is the audience you're targeting right for your service? With a poorly established campaign, this happens often!

MULTI-CHANNEL ATTRIBUTION

Multi-channel attribution is the process of looking at all your different marketing channels—email, paid ads, organic search—and identifying the multiple touch points at which a user interacts with your brand before finally converting into a lead/sale.

A sale doesn't usually happen through a single click. No one sees your ad once and decides right away they want to buy from you. The internet makes it easy to research, read reviews, and see multiple options before anyone decides that they want to purchase from you. Remember, the more expensive your product or service is, the more research and thought the user will put into the purchase. They'll Google you. They'll look on Wikipedia. They'll read reviews. They'll click on your ads. They'll check out your social media.

So, before you decide if a campaign is performing well or if a specific channel is bringing you good results, you have to look at the user's journey.

Let's say you have a very high conversion rate for your brand campaign. Are these only users that know you from somewhere else, and they just Googled your name right away? Or did they research you for a week or two before they finally decide they trust your brand? Maybe they searched for "where to buy kombucha." They checked your website along with some competitors. Then, they decided to narrow down their search to "organic kombucha." They find you organically, then later they Google your brand name directly, click on the ad and purchase!

Should all the credit go to the brand search, because it was the term they searched before purchasing? No, because if they hadn't seen your ad for "where to buy kombucha" in the first place, they might never have found your website and wouldn't have considered buying from you.

CONVERSION RATES & TRANSACTION VALUE

Great engagement is always a good sign, but is it directly correlated with your sales? Great engagement doesn't always mean good return on investment.

Analytics gives you data on how much you've spent and how much you've gotten back. If you're tracking events and goals, you need to know how much each of them is worth to you, and do the math from there. If you have e-commerce tracking, Analytics will tell you how much money you've made.

A good conversion rate can be anywhere from 1% (for high value products) to 7-10% (for smaller sales, form submissions, or calls).

Same as with engagement, check your conversion rate between campaigns and channels. Don't just look at the averages. See which campaigns give you the highest revenue, which landing pages perform better, and keep testing if you see lower performance for some of them.

MEASURING BRANDING

Branding is one of the most difficult parts of marketing to measure, primarily because of the necessary air gap between the the work and the results.

It's a terrible idea to have direct call-to-actions for a sale within your branding (nothing erodes trust more, especially in today's market), so without a common thread to track a user from first contact to purchase, it can be difficult to gauge branding's effectiveness. Yet, it's not impossible; it really just requires some common sense and observation of the marketplace.

One of the first ways that a digital brand can measure the effectiveness of their branding is by tracking direct brand mentions, direct website visits, searches, and organic follows. A well-designed branding campaign won't tell the audience to buy the product now, but it will stick in their minds, and if they want to buy the product later, they'll either mention the name on social media, follow the brand on Facebook, search Google for the website, or type the website URL in directly. All of these metrics can be measured independently of one another and correlated with branding efforts.

If you're promoting original content through your campaign, you can use unique tracking identifiers in your URLs in order to identify the source of the traffic (for example, promoting a post on Facebook which links to an article on your company's blog).

If your brand is large enough, you'll also be able to track hashtag usage or mentions on social channels like Instagram or Twitter.

ROI, ROAS, & COST DATA

When running any campaign, you will need to calculate your Return On Investment (ROI). Let's dive in with some real numbers.

If you want to calculate just your Return On Advertising Spending (ROAS) without overhead cost, the formula is: *ROAS = Total Revenue from Ads / Total Ad Cost.*

So, if you spent $1,000 on your campaigns in one month and generated a revenue of $5,000, then your return would be $5000 / $1000 = $5. That means that for every $1 spend on ads, you get $5!

Then, you probably want to calculate your ROI. The formula for ROI is *(Total Revenue From Ads − Total Cost)/Total Cost.* Business overhead eats up a bit of your actual profits. If you spent $1,000 on your campaigns in one month and generated a revenue of $5,000 with a business overhead cost of $2,000, then your return would be (5000−(1000+2000) / (1000+2000))*100% = 2000/3000*100% = 66.67%. This means that for every $1 of total cost, you got $1.66 in profit.

CASE STUDY: IMPROVING HOMEPAGE CONVERSIONS BY 28.6% THROUGH A/B TESTING

During our analysis of a client's website performance, we realized that homepage conversion was a problem. The primary purpose of their website was signing up new users for their web app, and we thought we could improve the conversion rate for this process.

The current website was built on an outdated Wordpress template. It was narrow, non-responsive, and felt too corporate. The images felt like stock images, and there were 5 calls-to-action immediately visible.

We redesigned the homepage to feel wider, newer, and responsive for mobile devices. Instead of stock images, we added high-quality photos that felt natural and authentic. We also removed distractions, simplifying the site down to 1 primary call-to-action.

Our hypothesis was that these strategies—simplifying, modernizing, and defining the message—would increase conversion rates. We decided to test the new page concurrently with the old in order to prove our hypothesis. We set up Google Analytics experiments (you can access this by going to Reports > Behavior > Experiments) to set up an A/B test. The old page's home was on the original link, and the new page's home was on a new URL (not indexed by Google) called /homepage.

(You can also use Google's free analytics tool called Optimize. Other tools to consider are screen recording apps like Hotjar, for watching user behavior on site).

We set the experiment to run for 2 weeks. We directed 25% of the site traffic to our A/B experiment. Of these, half were shown the new page and half the old page. Then, after seeing good results in the first 6 days, we started sending 50% of the site traffic to the new page. The first 6 days of the test saw a conversion rate for the new home page that was 101.22% higher than the old one. Bounce rate improved by 44.71%. The average number of pages people visited per session improved by 11.03%. The CTA (call to action) click-through rate on the homepage improved by 25.63%.

By the end of the two-week experiment, results stabilized and we saw these final numbers comparing the new home page to the old one:

- The conversion rate was 28.6% higher
- The bounce rate was 19.8% lower
- Time on page was 6% higher
- Users were 15.4% more likely to click on the CTA in the top banner

We made a few small adjustments for search indexing in the content of the page, and published the page, making it live for 100% of visitors. The result was a drastic increase of product signups for the client.

Learning how to track performance can be the difference between a mediocre marketing campaign and an amazing marketing campaign. That's why the skills covered in this chapter are so important: being able to report and accurately detail every dollar spent on a campaign definitely helps a marketer succeed with clients and other departments within their companies.

PART II:
SOFT SKILLS

IT'S NOT WHAT YOU KNOW, IT'S HOW YOU DO IT

"Tell your story before someone else tells it, because they will get it wrong."
- Jack Shock

After spending most of this book so far sharing all the hard skills that you need to know, I must now tell you that they actually aren't all that important. I'm exaggerating a bit, of course, but there's a shred of truth. The specific tactics and hard skills essential for being a successful marketer change all the time—fast enough, probably, that in five to ten years, this book will be obsolete.

However, I don't think this second part of the book will be obsolete, and that's because soft skills are eternal. They don't change. You need them for everything, not just marketing. In the end, a marketer is just a storyteller, and as a marketer, you are there to help people own their stories.

I didn't pay a lot of attention in most of college, unfortunately, but a few gems stuck in my mind. Dr. Jack Shock served as the White House Director of Presidential Letters and Messages during the Clinton Administration, and teaches public relations and communication law at my alma mater. That's where I was introduced to one of those gems. "Tell your story before someone else tells it," Shock says, "because they will get it wrong."

As a marketer, your job is to tell that story before anyone else does. Your job, even as a paid ads consultant or a social media intern, is to be the PR agent that stands in between a client and the public, making sure that you're crafting a message that improves your client's brand. You're selling things through stories.

There are just a few tricks to keep in mind.

First, specialization. It's not so much a soft skill as it is a looming fact: it's really hard to be successful without being excellent at something. If you're always just halfway to excellence, your career will be difficult. So, it's important to get an idea of where you want to be, what you're good at, and have a running list of strengths and weaknesses so you know where you stand.

Second, professional communication. You'd think that in the world of marketing, which is all about communicating, we'd have a lot of excellent individual communicators. Not true. Learning how to talk, express yourself, write well, be succinct, and get your point across is a very important set of soft skills.

Third, writing emails. It's a subset of professional communication, of course, but being a person who can write legible, personable, and efficient emails will set you apart from all of those who use email like SMS.

Fourth, time management. This isn't as much about saving time as knowing how to prioritize it. You'll always have to spend time on important things, but it's easy to get sidetracked, and to let others sidetrack you as well.

Fifth, sales. It's a word that makes people stiffen up, but if it weren't for sales, you probably wouldn't have a job. Being good at it (or at least knowing how to talk to someone) can be the difference between getting a $1,000 contract and a $100,000 contract.

And finally, economics. What? We're not economists here! Perhaps not, but understanding return on investment and how your marketing clients (whether that's the sales department, a small business owner, or your corporate consulting client) see income and expenses is essential to giving them the best value. Because, after all, if you're not making them money, they're not going to keep paying you.

SPECIALIZATION & BEING THE BEST AT WHAT YOU DO

In order for your work and your career to succeed, there has to be something about you—something you do, something you know, something you try—that is better than everyone else.

That's not to say you have to be the world's best at everything. Nobody is the absolute best (some people really are the world's best at almost everything, but they're the outliers) but almost anyone can become excellent at one thing. And most of us don't have to compete with the whole world—we just have to compete within our own little worlds: the worlds of our geography, language, community, and business market.

But the concept stands: in order to succeed, there's got to be something that you're doing better than your competitors. Otherwise you will not stand out. You don't want to be a generalist. You don't want to be kind-of-good at a lot of things, because then you will make kind-of-good money and have kind-of-good clients, and probably kind-of-bad stress levels.

If you look at any successful entity—whether it's an international fast food chain, a country, a local coffeeshop, or a car brand—they're where they are because they did something better than those around them. Perhaps McDonald's didn't make the healthiest or tastiest food, but they did do something better: the best logistics and food preparation process, lowering costs, and increasing predictability. Perhaps BMW didn't make the cheapest car, but they did do something better: focusing on performance, comfort, and quality. Perhaps Switzerland didn't make it especially easy or cheap to live within its borders, but it did build a rich and successful country with an amazing quality of life. Perhaps the coffeeshop doesn't make the cheapest coffee, but it does offer a better experience and vibe than the Starbucks down the street.

As a marketer, you've got to do something better. You can be sort-of-good at all facets of marketing, but unless there is one area you are really excellent in, you'll just be a sort-of-successful marketer. That's why you find incredibly successful people working in very tiny niches. Guerrilla marketing for toilet manufacturers? There's someone out there. Paid digital advertising for Arctic tour providers? There's someone out there. Search engine optimization for energy drink companies? Ditto.

I think that most people start as generalists in marketing, but those with long and successful marketing careers end up as specialists. You might start as a humble intern interested in agriculture, but twenty-five years later, you might be the go-to branding specialist for American dairy producers. You can pick from many things to become the best at. You can be the best within a very specific niche. You can be the best at optimizing fashion e-commerce websites. You can be the best at client networking. Each aspect you can think of counts as something that you can be better at than anyone else in your world.

Specialization is hard, and it's almost impossible to do right out of the gate, but I think that the sooner you can find the specialty you connect with, the sooner you'll find rewarding success in your career.

It's also worth noting that you don't have to wait until you're a high-level executive within a global marketing agency to be the best. You can be the best right where you are. You can be the best intern, or the best freelancer, or the best creative director—just find some aspect of your current work that sets you apart, and make sure you're truly, actually producing some of the best results in your circle.

PROFESSIONAL COMMUNICATION

I'm going to be entirely honest: I didn't really want to write this section for a multitude of reasons. First, because I have a lurking fear that I'll come across as an old codger. Second, I know I am not the most professional communicator (we'll get into why, later). And third, I realize that things change with time, and nobody can prophesy exactly what happens next.

Professional communication is about respect. Not the swagger sort of respect—it's not about demanding recognition and status. But neither is it the self-deprecating sort of hierarchical sort of respect, because it works both ways. It's more about recognizing that you're one half of a business relationship, and you'll do your best to make everyone's job easier, more efficient, and more honest and transparent. In my experience, the most important factors of professional communication are all about respect. These include promptness, accuracy, clarity, politeness, and straightforwardness.

Promptness is a respect for time. It's an acknowledgement that someone is depending upon you for information, and you will get it to them as soon as possible. For many years, the unwritten rule has been that a professional email deserves a response in under 24 hours. I think that's a fairly normal standard, and one that isn't too onerous to uphold. Same with a phone call or any other form of message: if you don't respond within a single business day, you're probably too late. But as always, everything has priorities. Even if you're busy, some things require an instant response. When a deal is on the line, or a project for a large client is extremely urgent, twenty-four hours might be too long. When it's important, it's important, so I try to make the time for it.

Accuracy and clarity are respect for decision-making. When you're passing information along to another party, whether you're chatting on the phone or sending an email, you want to convey everything as accurately as possible. This is a respect for their decision-making abilities: if they have accurate information, they'll be able to make the right call accordingly.

Politeness is respect for the other as a person. It's pretty amazing how much this differs according to industry, region, age, or mode of communication, but it's still extremely important. There isn't a standard measure of "yes sir" and "no ma'am" and "thank you so much" that is required in a discussion; rather, it's more of an awareness of the cultural expectations of your working relationships. Some people will be direct, while others will make small talk before getting down to business. Mirror their comfort level, chat with them if they want to chat, or start hammering business details out if they want to do so. I think that impoliteness starts when one party refuses to adjust to the other's comfort level. You've probably seen this before in some manner. It applies to all ages and cultures, and it goes in all directions—it's not just old stuffy guys talking down to young interns. It can also be a young guy trying to flex his business muscles in front of the old guys.

Straightforwardness is a respect for honesty. Although it should be obvious that outright lying doesn't have any place in decent business, there's a remarkable lack of straightforwardness in the world. This can be anything from glossing over some poor metrics in a report, to handily forgetting to convey some crucial performance information because it's embarrassing, or being shifty about billing or payment expectations.

All of the above is why I think professional communication, in a nutshell, is just about respect. Now, like I mentioned earlier, I'm aware that I'm not always the most professional communicator. Partially because we work in a tech-driven sphere where CEOs wear cargo shorts and cuss like sailors, and partially because I haven't worked in an office for about a decade and have consequently forgotten how to behave around normal people. I'm extremely casual. I also have a strong disregard for corporate America, so I'm probably overreacting to the guy in khakis with an MBA typing important, spreadsheety things on his ThinkPad.

WRITING EMAILS

Email is the currency of business communication. It remains the only universally adopted form of contact on the internet. You can't sign up to a single platform without it. Even Facebook tried to create an emailless login service, but it actually just gives you a

Facebook email address. If you can't write a good email, you're stuck. A poor email is like getting a phone call throughout which the other person is coughing and stuttering. Thankfully, it's not hard to write good emails.

A good email is:

Correct Language Usage. An email should use basic good English: correct grammar, appropriately capitalized letters, correct spelling, punctuation, and your basic three-part structure (sign on, message, sign off).

Clear. Don't beat around the bush. It's not a magazine article, it's a short letter to someone. It's not the time for flowery language or abstract thoughts.

Succinct. Say hi. Tell the person what you want to say. Then, say bye. It doesn't have to be more complicated than that. Use bullet points if you need to.

Not an SMS. It's not a one-line message. Don't use text speak or abbreviations. You can probably use emojis or text smileys these days, if you know the person, but it's still business, not getting drinks with your friends.

Self-contained. It's not a text. It's better to put everything in one message rather than follow it up with a string of half-completed thoughts. Save that for your texts, after you've had too many drinks with friends.

I get a lot of emails—from coworkers, clients, colleagues in the industry, job applicants, businesses. Each has their own unique flavor of appropriate structure and vibe. Maybe it's just because I get so many, but the proportion of poorly written emails seems like it's getting worse every year. Being able to write clearly and professionally will set you apart.

TIME MANAGEMENT

There are eight or nine hours in a typical workday. In how many of those do you think you actually get something done? By get something done, I mean actual, truly productive work.

Maybe four or five hours, if you're honest. The reality is that the amount of time spent working doesn't matter, and in most cases, nobody else cares how long your butt is in the chair, unless your results are less than stellar. As long as you're getting results, how long it takes to get them is largely irrelevant.

The issue of time management really only becomes important when you've got a high level of responsibility for outcomes. As an entry-level employee anywhere, chances are you're doing routine tasks that don't require a lot of independence or critical thought. We've all been there. The first couple years out of college are the years in which you've just got to grind through your tasks and prove you can handle some actually important decisions on your own. But pretty soon, you'll find out that as your level of responsibility grows, so does your independence, and with that comes the really important need for time management.

When you're a mid-level employee, or a freelancer, or the owner of an agency, or a consultant, you're suddenly faced with an onslaught of choices. The intern needs help figuring out your pipeline, clients are calling, a few meetings are scheduled, you've got a problem with billing, and on and on.

This is where time management becomes important. Yet, at the same time, proper time management is unique to every person and situation. There is no magic time to wake up, no magic way to make a meeting happen faster, no magic method of getting more done in an hour. You can either say yes or no to opportunities. Anyone who says differently is is likely selling something.

The first cardinal rule of time management is that meetings are dead time. In our cumulative decades of work, neither Anya or I have ever been a part of a regularly scheduled meeting that added value or clarity to our work. Sometimes meetings are imperative, but that's only when there's an active problem that needs solving and requires some heads to gather around a table.

A meeting doesn't just take an hour. It takes days. Say you've got an hour-long weekly meeting at ten o'clock on Tuesday, and four members of a team go to this meeting. Not only do you need to prepare for this meeting (for maybe fifteen to thirty minutes) but you've also got to block off time before and after the meeting (maybe another fifteen to thirty). Not to mention the distracting break from focus that an upcoming meeting imposes—always having to keep an eye on the clock, the impending meeting in the back of your mind. Then, you've got the meeting itself and any follow-ups it requires. Suddenly, multiply by four, and you've got an entire work day devoted to a meeting.

And what did that meeting accomplish? Nothing. Nobody wanted to be there except the person in charge of the meeting.

At Discosloth, we consciously made the decision to ban meetings. Not all meetings, of course, because sometimes you've got to talk with clients and make some sales, but we refuse to hold any regularly scheduled meeting. That's because if any information really needs to be distributed, we can do that with the amazingly effective medium of an email. If anyone needs to discuss something, we can pick up the phone and talk about it.

Although many companies still require meetings, and you might not be able to do much about it, any time spent in a meeting is time not spent working. So, avoid them as much as possible.

We've found that many agencies also spend countless hours onboarding clients, with meeting after meeting to discuss project scope, metrics, strategy, and progress. I'm not really sure why—it's very costly for the client, and unless you're handling a six- or seven-figure contract with a multinational, there's not a whole lot of need for ongoing meetings. We avoid it whenever possible, and we think productivity and happiness increases across the board when this happens.

The second rule is: don't get caught up in time spent working. Get caught up in focus and the quality of your ideas.

You'll see a lot of gurus with productivity hack methods—waking up at four in the morning, spending two hours at the gym, starting work at seven, working until six in the evening, doing some power squats, etc. I've worked with some of these people.

The reality is that these folks don't get a whole lot more done than I do, and I wake up at seven, have a relaxed breakfast and coffee, start work at nine, take an hour for lunch, work for a couple more hours in the afternoon, and that's about it. I work maybe four hours some days, twelve hours another day, but I try to make those extremely focused and productive.

A few years ago, I worked with a client who was all about energy. He had an obsession about something he called "peak state" which involved eating massive amounts of fruit in the morning (he did this instead of caffeine because fruit sugars were supposed to stimulate the brain), pushups, a thumping EDM playlist, and chugging massive amounts of water. We weren't filming a CrossFit training session. We were filming corporate videos about money management. It was a little bizarre, but I went with it. Hey—I try not to judge. As I continued working with this client, I was exposed to an entirely new world of what I can only describe as professional hustlers. It was a bizarre sort of salesman culture. Wake up at four. Eat fruit. Build a click funnel. Generate webinars. Do pushups. Gain high-net-worth clients. Make millions.

My relationship with this client didn't last long. Oddly, it didn't seem like he had enough liquid income to pay for marketing.

It made me wonder just how gullible people can be—and not just naive, desperate people, but also middle-class or upper-class professionals with disposable income and vacation homes.

It also made me realize that if you're actually at peak state, and are actually a high-achieving individual, you won't need to eat fruit and listen to Tiësto remixes to get there.

No billionaire became a billionaire because of a morning ritual.

SALES & ECONOMICS

Sales is a bad word for many marketers, but it doesn't mean what you think it means. It doesn't mean being a pushy used car salesman. It doesn't mean wearing a headset in a call center. It doesn't mean high-powered guys in suits. It just means knowing how to make money.

If you're working in marketing, you have to know sales. It doesn't matter whether you're the freshest intern or the CEO of a huge ad agency—you've got to sell yourself, your expertise, and your results, and make sure you get paid for it as well.

Sales has changed over the past few years, and even more so within the tech-forward industry of marketing. It's more about trust and relationships than ever before, and less about picking up the phone and making cold calls. It's more about your personal brand, and less about a sales process. As a matter of fact, if you listen to the wrong sort of advice and choose a sales process that is too impersonal or too aggressive, it can have a massively negative effect to your reputation, and ultimately, your long-term success.

Good sales means knowing your benefits and downsides, being honest about both, and getting in front of the people who need your services. It means efficiently communicating your value, covering the needs of your client, and ultimately getting a paycheck. Often, this comes in the form of providing valuable content or advice without charge—doing an audit for free, writing a detailed guide, making some strategy suggestions pro bono, or if you have a lot of time on your hands maybe even writing a book about becoming a digital marketer. Nickel-and-diming your clients isn't going to increase their confidence in your skills, but providing consistent value will.

Outreach is hard, and cold outreach is even harder. That's why I don't recommend cold emailing or cold calling as a worthwhile strategy for digital marketers to gain clients. The effective conversion rate will be microscopic. The more that your competitors cold call, the less effective it is. Some people are especially good at it, and kudos to them. Don't try to beat cold callers at their own game. Instead of playing the quantity strategy (calling thousands of businesses) play the quality strategy (find out where your ten already-interested clients are).

Networking, real in-person networking, is where the highest-value work is found. Having a beer with the decision maker in a company will result in better quality work with less client churn, so it's important to develop a personal relationship and pay for lots of their meals. Spending $100 now might seem costly, but after you get a $10,000 contract, it doesn't seem so bad.

When you hear "sales," it shouldn't bring to mind a scene out of Office Space. It should bring to mind developing relationships and providing value to your clients. What is value? It means bringing in more money than you cost. If you cost $1000 a month, but bring in $10,000 a month, they'll never get rid of you.

Which brings us to economics. It's a crucial aspect to consider when you're doing marketing for a client (or for a boss). Your entire existence and success as a marketer is brought about by bringing in more money than you're spending. It's the surest way to job security: if you can bring in more than you cost, you'll be fine.

Remember that gross sales aren't necessarily gross profit: your client has a lot of expenses to consider, including product cost, taxes, salaries, office space, advertising, and even your own compensation. It's often very hard to justify campaigns or projects to a client if they're costly but don't provide any directly tangible profits. And that's okay—if you can't prove your marketing work will result in better margins for the company, there's really no reason they should consent to spending more.

I asked Vlad Calus what he thought were important soft skills for the emerging marketer, and his responses were insightful. "Stay curious all the time," he said. "Understand why things are happening in a specific way and how you can improve it. Learn new things every day and week. Sign up for courses, read a blog, start your own, test, implement, iterate, and then try again. You're gonna fail a lot, and that's the beauty of it. There's always a lot of place for improvement. Build a marketing cycle. Get inspired from other industries like IT. Intel has a weekly content War Room that coordinates content, channels, and campaigns across audiences. Starbucks leverages a six-week work back plan across their social channels. Everything from the Pumpkin Spice Latte to the Red Cup campaigns go through this standard process. The New York Times has the famous "Page One" meeting two times daily to orchestrate a 24/7 news cycle. Wendy's has an impressive governance process that reviews everything from the table top merchandise to the video that comprises its drive-thru menu content. Think of ways you could fit in these teams."

We covered a few aspects of soft skills that are essential in furthering your marketing career: specialization, professional communication, writing emails, time management, sales, and economics. Explore all of these further, because mastering these is a long and ongoing process that will only make your career more fruitful and productive.

GETTING YOUR FIRST ENTRY-LEVEL DIGITAL MARKETING POSITION

"Existence can be beautiful or it can be ugly: but that's on you."
- Mr. Robot [8]

Between the two of us, we've worked as an employee in marketing-related fields for more years than we care to admit. Gil's first job out of college was as a marketing and social media intern at a nonprofit. After freelancing for almost five years, his next (and last) job was as a creative director at a company that sold round-the-world airfare.

Anya worked as a paid search specialist at a few companies, then ultimately ended up in her final nine-to-five job as the marketing manager for the same airfare company.

While we don't plan on going back to work for anyone, we recognize our employment experience was an important step towards being able to succeed in owning our own company, building various projects, and creating successful marketing endeavors. You've always got to start somewhere!

The reality of marketing is that, while working as an employee, you'll never make the same amount of money as employees in certain other fields. Someone in development or sales or pharmaceuticals will always make more as an employee. Within the United States, most creative and marketing positions will cap in the high five figures, unless you graduate into a VP or ownership role, and that's with twenty years of experience behind you.

However, it's difficult to just jump into freelancing or agency ownership without the support of a significant network or industry experience behind you, and that's why we think it's so important to get some solid experience working as an employee, whether it's in an in-house marketing or an agency position.

The good thing about marketing positions is that a little skill goes a long way. The field is ripe with positions that require just a little bit of extra skills than most marketers have; some study and hands-on practice with web development or media production can land you a very solid job in almost any market.

No longer do you only need to show up and be able to write an email: you also need to know how to wrangle a website, run ad campaigns, manage multiple social channels, and understand the elements of good public relations.

Going into your career with a backpack full of skills—whether soft skills or hard skills—is going to be the difference between a so-so job and an amazing job.

Something to remember is that the better the job, the easier it is. It's no secret that entry-level positions are miserable in a lot of ways. It makes sense: you've got no influence, you've got no purpose, you're making no money, and ultimately, your butt in the seat is infinitely replaceable. Making it past that initial entry-level job can get you to a place where you've got a bit more influence, purpose, money, and job security. But you can't just coast into these jobs: you've got to earn them. Typically, that just takes time!

Although we were once entry-level employees just like every graduate, in the decade or more since we were violently launched into career oblivion, we've hired people to help us with projects ranging from sales, software development, content creation, and media production.

As long as the person is moderately savvy and curious, hard skills are a minimal requirement. Degrees are a minimal requirement. Experience, too, is a minimal requirement. The most important requirements for a new hire are soft skills.

Networking. Being on time. Communicating clearly. Answering the phone. Taking initiative. Calling people when they need to solve a problem. Writing a quality email. Being able to make a risky decision.

None of these can be easily taught. Hard skills, on the other hand, can usually be taught. Things like learning HTML, or how to use a project management tool, or how to use Google Analytics, or how to edit a video. These are things that, while useful, are secondary to the soft skills that separate an average employee from a great employee.

What career paths are available for those wanting to work as an employee in a digital marketing function? Let's briefly go through a few of the most common.

Search engine optimization. One of the oldest forms of digital marketing, this is all about getting sites to appear organically in search engine results. It's crucially important for any company that has an online presence. This field rapidly changes, perhaps more than any other, since algorithms change every day. Sometimes it's a rat race to the bottom in order to get your site to the top, but it's also incredibly rewarding. It's a perfect choice for the highly technical who might not want to spend all of their time coding.

Paid advertising. For the first time ever, people are spending more time online than watching television—and ad revenue from digital has surpassed almost every other medium combined! The typical channels include Google Ads, Bing Ads, Facebook Ads, Instagram Ads, LinkedIn Ads, and the up-and-coming Amazon digital ad options. Paid advertising works closely with all sorts of others in marketing.

Content creation. This is a broad career path, perfect for the most creative. It can involve anything from copywriting, to video editing, to infographic creation, to photography. Because no matter how you publicize and amplify something, you've got to have something to show people. Good content is common: great content is rare.

Social media management. In a way, managing social media is a form of content creation, since you heavily rely on communicating both in word and in visuals, but it also includes elements of PR and branding. This is perhaps the most precarious position, since channels change and die off, and social media's return on investment for companies is growing smaller every year as platforms change their stance on outbound linking.

UX or branding design. As companies flock online, user experience (UX) and branding become essential to keep users on their sites. With unlimited other options, you want to be the best in the world so you don't lose clients and sales. UX design ensures optimum efficiency and profits, and branding is part of creating the story that attracts, and ultimately retains, new customers to your company.

Web development. None of marketing would even be possible if we weren't able to deploy our visions. That's where the web developer comes in. From the humble beginnings of webmasters in the 90s, to the slightly more technical web designers in the 00s, to the full-fledged frontend dev of today, it's a highly technical and also highly paid position that is in constant demand.

Public relations. Larger companies, especially those who aren't tightly run by their founders, can have a hard time telling their story. PR has evolved over the years, but the core importance is the same: take control of your own story, or others will tell it for you. A career in PR is perfect for the savvy professional who is great with networking, fearless at communicating, and can get things done like a hammer. Even traditional PR roles, like crisis management, now need to understand how the digital world communicates.

E-commerce sales. In a world where online physical sales are eclipsing normal brick and mortar retail, an e-commerce specialist will be in increasingly high demand. Familiarity with e-commerce platforms like Shopify and WooCommerce, along with all the associated practices like running PPC, SEO, and paid social campaigns, is essential. A thorough understanding of analytics will help nail down effective strategies.

Analytics and data. Speaking of effective strategies, the data-oriented among us will find a perfect fit in an analytics role. Taking large amounts of user data and translating it into something the business people understand is a vital part of running a digital company, and more employers are looking for those who can fill this role.

All-round marketing manager. More often than not, companies are looking for what they simply term a "marketing manager." Especially if a company can't afford an entire department, or can't afford to outsource everything to an agency, they will hire a jack-of-all-trades person to manage things like paid ads, SEO, content creation, website maintenance, and a million other little things. If you're good at a lot of things, perhaps this is a perfect choice for you.

WHAT HAPPENS WHEN LUCRATIVE JOBS BECOME COMMODITIZED?

For the past decade or two, the new conventional wisdom has been that STEM jobs—science, technology, engineering, and mathematics jobs—are the way to go if a young graduate wants a stable and lucrative career. While this is still greatly true, I think that, in the long-term, we are going to see a reduction in the upside of these vocations. It's important for the aspiring marketer to remember that jobs are being speedily commoditized, and to know how to future-proof himself.

Why are jobs being commoditized? They're simply becoming so commonplace that rarity no longer creates value.
We've seen patterns like this in the past. For many years, practicing law was one of the most respected and lucrative careers that a young American could aspire to. While it's still very possible to make good money from a law career, it's limited to the top tier of litigators and principals that are able to make an envious level of cash. The average starting compensation for a lawyer is $84,111. This seems low considering the average cost for law school has been hovering around $81,200, and requires a total of seven years of secondary education.

On top of this, employment rates for law school grads have been falling for the last decade, with rates lower than 84%. There are simply too many—and the number of law schools is ever increasing.

This isn't to say that I think that either law or computer science is a bad career choice. I'm just of the opinion that it's becoming commoditized, and the era of young developers or marketers making $200k might be drawing to an end. The proliferation of coding boot camps has generated a surge of low-level developers that go into coding-level jobs (mostly web design). The ease of access to the internet has created millions of potential marketers out there, learning how to build websites and run ad campaigns. It's my opinion that enough people have the desire to go into programming and marketing that it's going to become as commoditized as law, nursing, or accounting has become.

I think there are a few takeaways for people in the tech world to consider. First, pure tech skills alone are relatively unimportant. What is more important is harder to train: critical thinking, creativity, business savvy, and innovation. The successful developers and marketers I know aren't necessarily coding or branding gods. They're just really good at applying their skills to a product within a business environment.

Second, every career, even marketing or advertising, will require more and more technological prowess. I'm not even in a development career, but I write code, use Git, and run scripts every week.

Third, it's easy to fetishize the glamorous instead of the practical. That's why I see a lot of people heading to hipster hotspots for fancy-sounding but low-paying jobs, where the cost of living outpaces their salary, and then having an identity crisis a couple years later and switching to medical equipment sales where they can make $300,000 a year.

Fourth, wherever there is a glut, there is an equal and opposite absence. Somewhere, there is an industry that needs your skills. It might be in toilet manufacturing. Who knows?

GURUS, NINJAS, & WEBINARS: THINGS TO IGNORE

Things change fast in marketing. New techniques pop up every day, and if you're not careful, your marketing efforts can swiftly be derailed into never-ending rabbit holes of growth hacks, processes, fancy trends, and must-try ideas.

While it's always a good thing to test new marketing methods, it's important to remember that nothing worth doing is easy. And usually, when someone promises results that are instant, free, easy, or exponential, it's overhyped. Don't listen to the hustle and grind lifestyle marketer gurus: they're just selling an expensive online course. A healthy dose of skepticism goes a long way in marketing!

Of course, naming off individual strategies won't help much, since there are always new questionable techniques coming to surface, so instead, let's take a look at the symptoms of bad marketing advice. What specifically makes a strategy something to ignore?

Instant results. If you've been promised instant results (or super-fast, almost-instant results), there's a huge chance that the strategy is bunk. Why? The simple answer is that good things take time. Nothing happens overnight—and anyone who says differently is either an outlier, or selling something.

Free results. Similarly to instant results, you shouldn't trust a strategy that promises free results. Nothing is truly free: if you're not paying for results with cash, you can expect an equal outlay of time and labor. Sure, many things can be done without paying someone else or spending money on a single ad, but you've got to spend significant time on anything that doesn't cost. And "significant time" in this industry isn't just a few days of work. It's probably more like months and months, if not years.

Easy results. The problem with easy strategies is that everyone can do them: and if everyone starts doing them, they stop working. It's the law of supply and demand: if success was as simple as posting a status to Facebook, then every one of the billions of people on that platform would be successful. Good strategies require expertise, hard work, and sometimes money to spend on it. If it feels too good to be true, it is.

Risk-free results. Here's where return vs. reward comes into play. It's like comparing a bank savings account with a high-yield corporate bond: the first is much more safer, but offers a lot less interest than the second. You are always risking something when you're trying a new strategy: whether that's time, money, energy, reputation, or trust.

Exponential results. In almost every case (there are always exceptions), you shouldn't put too much stock into marketing strategies that promise exponential results. Most good strategies offer logarithmic results—put a certain amount of money in, get a certain amount of money out. Tweet a certain amount of times, get a certain amount of leads. The exceptions are outliers: sometimes you can tweet and get 100,000 retweets, but don't expect to replicate that.

Often, the creation of a new platform creates the most over-hype in the marketing world. For example, a few years back the livestreaming platform Periscope launched. Marketers in all sorts of industries flocked towards it in a frenzy. They added Periscope icons on their websites and moved their podcasts over to it. Courses were swiftly written, filmed, and launched in order to teach people how to get thousands of followers and make millions of dollars. The platform was popular for about five months. Today, I don't know of anyone who actually uses Periscope. It's the same with pop marketing terms like chatbots, AI, conversational marketing, growth hacking, and so on.

In the end, there are many ways to see success, using all sorts of strategies—but all of them require work, and none of them actually require a whole lot of specialized knowledge. You just need time, energy, and some patience.

You definitely shouldn't pay someone a thousand bucks to download a guru course on inbound funnels!

WRITING YOUR RESUME: THESE LABELS HAVE BEEN DEPRECATED

Entrepreneur. Storyteller. Maker. Polymath. Multipotentialite. I've looked at a lot of resumes lately. I've seen some terms used over and over and over. I'm here to encourage those recently (or not-so-recently) graduated aspiring marketers to avoid the catchphrases and instead focus on what you're good at.

Storyteller. I bring this one up first because I am most guilty of this label. See, when I graduated from college seven years ago, this word was in trend. It was hot. In reality, I was only 21-year-old fresh meat with little sense and even less experience. The term "storyteller" was something that seemed to encapsulate what I wanted to be. What I didn't grasp is that no one is going to pay you to be a storyteller. They're going to pay you to make them money.

A couple years ago, I combed through dozens of resumes, looking for an entry-level candidate for a social media position. I realized that most graduating seniors have 1) almost all used the term "storyteller" on their resume, and 2) been surrounded by social media for their entire adult lives. A college kid who graduates in 2017 was only ten years old when Facebook came around. They're too close to it to see social for what it is: simply a stage on which to hawk your wares.

That's it. It's not your life. It's just a stage.

Earning the title of "storyteller" takes a little more than managing a company's social media account, writing some SEO-worthy articles for a clothing boutique, or posting a witty comment about your favorite podcast.

I can think of a few people I know who have earned the title of "storyteller." Journalists who flew into Sudan in a Piper Cub. Someone's grandmother telling stories from the thirties. An old man smoking a cigarette at a coffeeshop. People who worked for Clinton. Liberian Ebola doctors.

You shouldn't call yourself a storyteller. Let others call you that.

Entrepreneur. Like the term "storyteller," this is another term not to use on yourself. Someone else has to introduce you as this: otherwise, you're grandstanding. Let's go over what an entrepreneur is not.

First, it's not being self-employed. 10.1% of the American workforce is self-employed. Self-employment is not uncommon.

Second, it's not being a freelancer. There are 55 million people in the United States who freelance in one form or the other. I freelanced for almost five years, and I knew for sure that I wasn't an entrepreneur.

Third, it's not selling with MLM. An incredible 99.7% of people selling things from Amway, Plexus, Avon, Arbonne, and Herbalife never recoup their initial investment. The rest of them, that remaining 0.3%, are simply on top of the pyramid.

Fourth, it's not just visualizing a startup. Worldwide, each year there are around 300,000,000 people attempting to startup approximately 150 million businesses. And 9 out of 10 of people who try to enter self-employment will fail within five years.

So, just like drinking coffee and playing with WordPress themes doesn't make you a developer, simply organizing an LLC and getting an Amex business card doesn't make you an entrepreneur. An entrepreneur is one who really stands out from the pack and builds something new—and successful. I'm talking about the 1 out of 10 businesses that doesn't fail.

Chances are, if you call yourself an entrepreneur you're not. Millions of people have gone before you proclaiming entrepreneurship. It's a badge of honor that must be bestowed, not claimed.

Maker. I'm glad that this one is falling out of vogue, because I think it's an anachronism. What "makers" are now—guys who solder together Arduino boards and have a 3D printer—are what the majority of the world was only a couple generations ago. In our grandfather's era, skills like carving, forging, soldering, plumbing, and casting were simply what they did when they showed up to work.

I think the ability to create something by combining technology is a lovely thing. It's a hobby of my own: soldering guitar pedals or swapping transmissions or fiddling with old Commodore

64s. But it's not something to put on the resume unless you're an electrical engineer or a hardware architect. It's simply called being handy.

Polymath. A polymath is, by definition: "a person whose expertise spans a significant number of different subject areas; such a person is known to draw on complex bodies of knowledge to solve specific problems."

Or, in other words, it's about the same as "jack of all trades, master of none."

When I graduated, I didn't have much experience in the world. Nobody does. But describing yourself as a generalist, a polymath, or a jack of all trades is a sure way to a career of mediocrity. A handyman who is kind of good at anything handy will barely be able to support himself. Someone who specializes in repairing high-end air conditioning systems will make $250,000 a year.

The phrase "jack of all trades, master of none" has an equivalent in almost every language. In Russian, it's "He can sew, mow, and play the flute." In Lithuanian, it's "When you have nine trades, your tenth one is famine." And in Cantonese, "knives all over, yet none is sharp."

Being a polymath isn't something to be proud of, unless you're Richard Branson and can pilot boats, balloons, and rocketships.

Multipotentialite. I've saved the best for last. I did not know this was a real word used by real people, until I floated out the word that I was looking for a freelance content creator. A gentleman introduced me to a young lady who seemed bright and ambitious. But then I took half a look at her resume and she lost all potential. No pun intended.

This candidate described herself as a multipotentialite. I did a double take and headed straight for Google. Unfortunately, multipotentialite seems to be an actual word that's caught on. It essentially means "I'll be a polymath...eventually." It means "I want to be good at stuff, but I'm not quite there." I don't think many people are out there using multipotentialite as a selling point on their resume, but just in case, here's a word of friendly warning: *don't*.

People want to see who you are. What you've done. How you present yourself. Whether you're hardworking. And most importantly, whether they like you.

Because, believe it or not, if you want a job, you're only going to get it if people like you: skills, education, and experience be damned. If you're likeable, you're going to blow the other candidates out of the water.

A stuffy resume will get you a stuffy job. If that's your drift, then go for it. But if you imagine yourself to be a storyteller, entrepreneur, maker, polymath, or multipotentialite, then by all means, go out and do those things so that people start calling you by those names. The resume is irrelevant. Make *yourself* your resume.

Working As A Freelancer In Marketing

"A woodpecker can tap twenty times on a thousand trees and get nowhere, but stay busy. Or he can tap twenty-thousand times on one tree and get dinner." [9]
- Seth Godin

You've seen the photos on Instagram: a laptop balanced on a pair of well-tanned legs that may look slightly like hot dogs. In the background, the surf crashes on an ivory beach.

It may not seem achievable, but location independence is becoming more and more common: sick and tired of a life spent inside a cold, grey cubicle, workers are breaking out of the norm and deciding to work from wherever they want.

It's not always easy, but it's very doable. When I was right out of college, I was told two different things by mentors: some told me to do what I love, and others told me to do what paid well. I asked Vlad Calus, the cofounder of Planable who has been self-employed since his teenage years, for his take on this advice.

"Do what you love and what gets you paid," was his response. "When you're young you don't have many responsibilities to the world—kids, house, bills. I believe that's the best time to experiment, play, try, and don't be afraid to fail. You can save a lot of money by staying at your parents until you figure out stuff. And the most important thing—none of us knows what we're doing. And if you think you want to do something that you're passionate about, make sure to figure a way to get paid well for that. It's important to stay happy doing what you love, but it's also important to pay bills and have food on the table. "

And he's right. For five years, I worked as a freelancer in the field of marketing. I was sort of a generalist, and not always in a good way. Most of the time, I did whatever paid—email marketing, web design, advertising, and other things, although throughout that five years I gradually narrowed my focus to animation, video editing, photography, and film production. I worked for a wide range of clients with a heavy emphasis in NGOs (non-governmental organizations) which let me travel extensively throughout all sorts of interesting parts of the world.

When I graduated college, I didn't really think about location independence or freelancing as an option. The term "digital nomad" wasn't really a catchphrase yet, and Instagram was barely a thing. I always liked to travel, but I didn't really think of it as a sustainable option for a career. So, I did the responsible thing and got a normal job, an entry-level marketing position at a nonprofit on the East Coast.

It was a nice job, but it paid zilch ($27,000 a year, to be exact). And eventually, as a college graduate making a salary far below average American wage, yet really wanting to buy a motorcycle, I decided I had to do something about it.

I quit the job at the nonprofit and started freelancing, doing the same things I was doing at the 9 to 5. Video production, branding, animation, photography, web design, marketing consulting —a really disorganized grab bag of a career. Located in the middle of Arkansas, I wasn't especially stimulated, so I began reaching out for nonprofit gigs that required travel. From contacts I'd made both at college and at my first job, those freelance gigs took me everywhere. India. Uganda. Kenya. South Africa. Costa Rica. And then, in 2014, one job took me to Liberia in the midst of the Ebola outbreak. I walked through the first Ebola unit in Liberia with a GoPro and a hazmat suit, interviewed the Time Magazine person of the year, and nearly got arrested by a trio of uniformed Liberian police who pulled me over while driving a Mitsubishi Pajero. It was a great experience, but it wasn't going in the right direction—I didn't think I was a great match for the demanding lifestyle of a photojournalist and filmmaker on the edge. I didn't want to spend my entire career holding a camera in sweaty places—so, I decided it was time to look for something else. I took a full-time job as a creative director, and that was where I met Anya.

Anya got a bachelor's degree in marketing and a master's in advertising, but right after college she realized that nothing she learned in school could be applied in the real world marketing of today. She tried to get a position at marketing agencies, but she didn't have any knowledge of current techniques. Nobody would take her, because she didn't have this real world experience.

She decided to do it her own way, and she started learning paid advertising by herself, helping other people with their clients as a freelancer.

Armed with this experience, she then worked as a paid advertising specialist, focusing on pay-per-click campaigns, especially Google Ads. She ran campaigns for travel companies, lumber companies, solo projects, and other businesses. She then became the paid ads specialist, and ultimately the marketing director, at the same company I worked at. After a couple years we both left—and started our own company!

THE IMPORTANCE OF SPECIALIZATION

A year or so ago, we reviewed applicants for an entry-level writing gig. The good news, for us, is that there were plenty of applicants—I paused the job posting after two days and 138 applicants, because I couldn't keep up with them all! The bad news, for applicants, is that the competition is fierce, and apparently every other communications or English major in North America is currently looking for a remote writing gig.

Looking through the resumes reminded us of our final semesters of college and the mad dash for employment. We sent out lots of resumes, applied for dozens of opportunities, and thankfully, some of them landed. But we did so many things wrong.

Hopefully, new graduates can learn from our experiences! Here are some of the problems we had when we first looked for post-graduation work:

Being too confident in the wrong things. Confidence is good. Misplaced confidence is just the worst. I thought I could do everything. I thought I was a polymathic digital god. I thought I was an animator, a content writer, a photographer, a web designer, a Javascripter, a social media manager, a video editor, a graphic designer. Turns out I'm none of those things. Those things themselves

167

are meaningless, in the long run. The fact that I had abilities in all those areas was good, but they are actually only symptoms. And these hard skills are things that thousands of other people do. I was confident in my creative abilities, my travel, my experiences, but there is always someone who is better at creating, has traveled more, and experienced more. These hard skills are not what will separate you from the rest of the industry.

What I actually do, and this is something that took years to figure out, is *sell things*. This is a dirty phrase to almost every creative and marketing professional out there, but it took a while to find out that this is actually what I was good at: selling myself to clients, and as a marketing strategist, selling my clients to others.

Not being confident enough in the right things. At the same time I was overly confident in the wrong things (the specific hard skills) I wasn't confident at all in the things I should have been: the soft skills. I did not think I was good at sales. I wasn't confident that I'd get a job; I did. Later, I wasn't confident that I could freelance; I did for five years. Even later, I wasn't confident I could start a company. Guess what? I did. I wasn't confident that I could talk to people, that I could incorporate a company, that I could pay my taxes, that I could make rent, that I could develop long-term business relationships. Those intangible skills, I learned later on, are the real value.

Not specializing. Many of the resumes we've seen are listing all these technical abilities and skillsets. But here's the deal: We don't want someone who's an expert at Photoshop, content writing, SEO, and also analyzing SQL datasets; we don't want a jack of all trades. We want someone who is an expert at one thing. Looking back, I thought I was an expert at everything. I was actually an expert in nothing. If someone asked me what I did, I couldn't answer in a sentence. And that was the biggest mistake of my first couple years out in the real world: I did too much.

I don't blame anyone for this, though. It takes time to find your niche. Start looking for your niche even within your initial entry-level jobs. It's part of growing into your career. It will be a huge boon if you can find this expertise early on.

Thinking I needed to follow my passion. As we looked over resumes, a few things jumped out. The first is that out of 138 applications, only 19 included everything we asked for in the job posting, making it easier to dump the other 119 into the digital trash bin. The second thing is that many of these entry-level applicants, fresh from college, are doing exactly what I was doing: following my passion. Passion is great, but I see a lot of people following what they think their passion is, only to learn they don't really feel fulfilled by it.

Going for cool instead of cash. I wanted to work with cool clients rather than building a profitable company with a sustainable business model. It took a couple years to realize that work is work. And if everybody wants to do something, the law of supply and demand means you're up against a lot of competition and razor-thin margins.

Now, at Discosloth, our daily routine is not exactly glamorous. We audit business websites for search engine marketing performance. We analyze ad channel ROI. We have long talks with clients on the phone. We spend most of our time in spreadsheets. But work is work. And you'll always be able to bring in a little of your hard skills and passion to play in any position.

GAINING CLIENTS AS A FREELANCER

If there was one thing that stands between every full-time marketer and freelance work, it would be the fear of not being able to gain enough clients, and for good reason: by far, it's the most difficult part of running your own show.

Your struggles with getting enough work will vary depending upon your background. If you're a fresh college grad with no work experience, it's nigh on impossible to find enough work to keep you going—you simply have no existing network to send work your way.

If you've been working for a decade or two, on the other hand, you've likely built up a significant base of contacts in your industry, and work can be sent your way as soon as you shoot an email out announcing your entry into the world of freelance.

Most often, freelancers worked at agencies for a time, and brought along some clients when they left. This is how the vast majority of freelancers and agencies start, and if you can manage to pull this off, you'll have a much easier time of it!

But, even with a long and distinguished professional background, the most well-networked of freelancers can have dry spells and need to onboard new clients. There are a million ways to do this, and chances are, you'll need to experiment with a few before you find the one that works for you.

Offline networking and events. One of the most tried and true methods, simply showing up to local events and creating a personal brand, can give you enough of a base to pay the bills. Local clients, while usually working with smaller budgets, have the benefit of being easily accessible and usually under-served. It's easy to make a big difference with a small, local client, and over time, your referrals will increase as they recommend you to their friends.

Social media. If you've got a big social following, use this to your advantage. The problem with this is that every other freelancer is also using this channel, because it's free and easy, and so you're easily lost in the crowd. In the end, you're sort of relegated to your offline network until you build up a significant brand. One thing to look out for are regularly scheduled weekly Twitter chats within your particular field of expertise. There are dozens of these in digital marketing—things like #seochat or #ppcchat, which you can pop into from time to time and start to be seen within the industry.

Paid advertising. Rarely attainable for freelancers because of cost, it's an option that still works for specific niches and those of you with larger budgets. Since you can easily target a narrow, highly defined audience, you can advertise directly to those who need your services at that specific moment.

Gig platforms. While it might sound questionable, a great opportunity to find new clients comes in the form of online gig platforms like Fiverr, UpWork, and similar smaller platforms. While it can take a long time to get established on these platforms, once your profile has a few ratings you can easily increase your prices and see a steady stream of inquiries.

Apply for remote/temporary jobs. Even looking on Craigslist can find you a steady stream of smaller jobs—usually one-time or very short-term. Even though they rarely pay well, if you're at the point where $50 is the difference between making rent and getting kicked out, it's worth the shot. You'll have to sort through a lot of crap to get to the good clients, but do this for a few months and you'll find a couple of clients worth doing repeat work for.

Cold calling. If you're a salesman, do this. It works. If you're like 95% of us, don't do this. It's scary. But if you can do it, more power to you! You'll make a lot of money. That said, I don't see a lot of marketers being successful at this. In today's world, I strongly believe that personal relationships will go much further than impersonal tactics.

Work for non-profit organizations. Sure, lots of people will tell you to never work for free. And it's usually a good idea. But sometimes, getting your foot in the door is invaluable. And once your work is seen and talked about, you'll discover that profit is in non-profits, after all. Once you've established your presence in a field, you'll find it so much easier to get more projects in the future.

PREPARING FOR JUMPING SHIP & GOING FREELANCE

So, despite all of the advice against going freelance, you've decided to give it a try. Congratulations! Regardless of your specific niche within the huge world of marketing, you've entered an entirely new level of responsibility and risk—and also some amazing reward. Hopefully, many such rewards will be monetary, so you can pay your bills, save up for the future, and expand your business. But even more than that, your reward will be an incredible amount of flexibility and independence that will let you take more control over your life and your time.

There are a few steps to take before you go freelancing. Preparation will make things go so much easier when you finally take the jump.

The first thing to consider is your financial situation. You can't expect to be making six figures right out of the gate—it will take time to onboard clients, set up some projects, and start getting paid. You'll find a host of people offering different viewpoints on how much you need to save. This number is very personal and contingent upon things like where you live, how lucrative your field is, how good you are at selling, how frugal you are, etc. I'd say an absolute minimum is three months worth of typical expenses, but that's cutting it close. When I first went freelancing, I had about six months of savings, and that wasn't very much. I had an incredibly slow first year and ate up most of those savings.

Sometimes, you may be advised that a little hunger is necessary to move you in the right direction—and yes, as a freelancer you soon develop a sort of gnawing hunger that pushes you beyond your comfort zone and makes you do things you wouldn't naturally do (like get on the phone with strangers, or send a proposal to new organizations). But it also can make you do things you shouldn't be focusing on in the grand scheme of things. My major mistake, during the first few years of my freelancing, was not focusing. But I couldn't focus. I needed to make money, now. Never mind that logo design wasn't what I wanted to do—$500 is $500. Trapped in an endless cycle of doing any random marketing work means that you can never get far enough ahead to say no to the projects that don't help your own personal strategy. I was copywriting articles, building websites, making videos, and becoming a jack-of-all-trades. I wasn't ever referred to as that "expert in filmmaking" but instead was "that marketing guy." The problem is, "that marketing guy" was just the guy you hire when you don't know what else to do. It's not bad, but it's not terribly lucrative either. As my friend Anna Packer said, it's another iteration of "good being the enemy of great."

The more you specialize, the better clients you get, the more you become an expert in your field, the easier it gets. However, it's hard to get to that level if you're unfocused, generalizing in all sorts of marketing work. Having a level of savings that lets you focus on building your place within your niche can be expensive up front, but much more stable over the long run. Just don't expect to be making your fortune the week after you start.

Another financial aspect to consider is debt: whether it's student debt, a car payment, a mortgage on your house, it's something that significantly increases your risk when going solo. Not only can it represent a large increase in your living expenses, but debt comes with negative repercussions if you don't pay it. It's one thing to be broke; it's another thing to lose your house. Both Anya and I were fortunate enough to graduate college with scholarships and then not take on a mortgage to worry about. I'm not sure we could have both freelanced, and then eventually started Discosloth, if we'd been suffocating under a load of debt.

Even without debt, living still costs! During the first eight months of freelancing, I fell back on the classic strategy of a part-time barista job, slinging coffee in the early mornings and late nights. Even working a few hours a week brought in an extra thousand dollars or so, which goes a long way when you're a 22-year-old living off of Totino's pizzas and fried rice. By the time I was about tired of making coffee for people, I'd developed enough freelance work to make it worth quitting.

The second thing to consider is your networking. If you've been working for any amount of time, you have developed contacts within each of your workplaces. The instant you quit your job and start freelancing, that naturally occurring network process goes away almost instantly. You don't just run into people who are in your field: in your first few months you will have to actively go out and find them. You have to find other people who are in your line of work and make the concerted effort to develop relationships with them. Sometimes this is from joint projects, sometimes it's just pint night at the local pub. Either way, you can't stay at home and expect to develop relationships in your industry. Go to events. Participate in fundraisers. Call people and have a beer. Ask around for others who are freelancing.

You should also consider your business process. By this, I don't mean build complicated business models and sales funnels to get business. It's easy to find guides that tell you to create lengthy business plans, multi-step processes, how to set up customer relationship systems, coming up with mottos and mission statements. That's needlessly complicating things, because in the real world you only have a few seconds to communicate what you do. If you can't express your business purpose in a single sentence, you probably don't understand it yourself. I was there, too, at one point. When I first started, I'd be asked what it was, exactly, that I did for a living. My answer was usually long-winded and all-encompassing, talking about marketing and websites and videos and social media and photography. By the end of my rant, people would get all glassy-eyed and file me away as "that media guy"—and that's not a very good brand to be filed.

Now, I can sum up Discosloth's purpose in a single statement: we do search marketing, and we help people advertise online. It's much more detailed, much more narrow, and much more effective.

What To Not Do

You should not start a blog. I'm just going to leave this one out there, for everyone to see. If it was 2003, it might be a different story.

But it's not. There are literally hundreds of thousands of blogs out there with starving writers thinking they'll be the next breakout blogger. This ship has sailed. Do not pursue this unless you are a sucker for financial pain.

You should not expect to relax on the beach. If anyone comes up to you and tells you that he's an entrepreneur and spends most of his two-hour workday on the beach, here's the reality: he's either broke or has a sugar daddy. Working for yourself, if you expect any level of success, will require long, cruel, sad, grueling hours.

You should not become an *internet marketer*. This is often code for "I can't hold down a real job and I don't have any hard skills so I will create inbound marketing funnels as my career." I can't tell you how many internet marketers I've met. They like to spout stuff about their HubSpot certification and "agile workflow" but there is no depth there. So be careful.

And finally, but perhaps most importantly, I try to discourage people from becoming a jack-of-all-trades. As we mentioned before, sometimes it's unavoidable as a young marketer just getting into the field. Perhaps you don't even know what you want or don't even know what's in demand, and in order to find out, you have to try it all. That's fine. But the sooner you specialize, the easier your work will be, the better you will be at it, and the more you will get paid.

Freelancing in marketing is hard, but it's getting easier every day. It's no longer required to be in the same physical location as most of your clients, which allows you to work with very low overhead and serve a wide range of clients. And if you take only one thing away from this chapter, remember to specialize: it's one of the best ways to set yourself apart from the hundreds of thousands of other freelance marketers in the world.

STARTING YOUR OWN MARKETING COMPANY

"If they give you ruled paper, write the other way."
- Juan Ramón Jiménez [10]

So you want to start your own marketing company!
What you're really saying is, I want to be in an industry where I'll have to market my own company amongst millions of the most experienced and skilled marketers in the world—other marketers. Sounds like you're a glutton for punishment! Before you embark on your journey of self-flagellation and self-employment, do your research.

A few years ago, I started writing a piece with the biased assumption that innovation was greater than ever. This assumption was based on anecdotal evidence, but it was wrong.

My assumption was wrong because I forgot that I live in a bubble. We all do. We are all surrounded by trappings of our own choice, and that's why so many bad decisions are made, every year, by so many of us.

Because I've been lucky enough to have some incredibly driven, smart, and highly motivated people around me, it was easy to assume that the world is always heading towards innovation in business, self employment, growth, and increasing revenue. While it usually does, at a macro level, it doesn't always do so on a micro level. I do still think we're heading towards decentralization in many ways (specifically, the separation from massive corporate conglomerates to personal, small business); however, I'm not sure the data I found actually supported my initial theory.

I headed over to Google Trends and ran some searches. While it's not the most scientific of studies, perhaps, I think it's an underrated way to gauge public sentiment. I chose the maximum possible time frame for results (from 2004-present) and limited them to the United States.

Some terms I wanted to search for (like "self-employment") weren't really applicable, since they are very seasonal, and see spikes every year around tax season. Many other terms don't see enough traffic for a rankings report, but I was able to find a few general terms that I thought reflect the amount of interest in going out on your own and starting a company: freelancer, starting a company, and starting a business.

The outlook wasn't good, and there was a strong correlation among them all. Interest in forging your own way seemed to be plunging. A 2016 article on CNN told me that new business startups in the United States were at a 40-year low.

Then I compared searches for "starting a company" with "fired from job." There was no correlation. This wasn't good. Not only is getting fired bad, but no correlating increase in innovation (starting businesses) means that employees are only cycling back into the same workforce that didn't work out for them in the first place.

Some of this might be regional (the US has seen very low comparative growth over the past 15 years as contrasted with emerging economies), as shown in a few searches I ran in other countries. I found that people in Singapore, Estonia, New Zealand, Australia, and Canada search the most for startup- or freelance-related terms, which did agree with my direct experience working with businesses across the world (our largest number of new client inquiries actually don't come from the US).

WHY WE SHOULDN'T SUPPORT SMALL BUSINESS

The heading is inflammatory, I know. I clickbaited it. We like small businesses. The vast majority of our hundreds of clients through the years have been small businesses. We are a small business!

There's been a lot of ground-swell around the need to support small businesses. It's a well-intentioned cause, and one that we truly agree with at the core. But it's dangerous to make the case for small business without an understanding of why many of them are struggling in the first place.

I don't think we should support a small businesses just because it's small. That sort of thinking—of putting money somewhere out of nostalgia rather than utility—is the reason they are are struggling in the first place.

If a small business wants to succeed, they've got to give their customers a valid improvement over what comes from the big guys. Sometimes, in the face of incoming conglomerates and multinationals, this means totally pivoting your business in order to fill a niche that Walmart can't.

A year or two ago, when we were back in the United States for a few weeks, we drove around with my dad, looking for a breakfast diner. We went to four old diner locations that he'd been to before, but every single one of these diners were closed down. It seemed a little ridiculous. At 9am on a Friday, we couldn't find somewhere to have bacon and hashbrowns. We were running out of time, and we had a flight to hop onto. We ended up at McDonald's.

There are a lot of reasons small businesses are struggling. Much of it has to do with the sputtering economy. But a lot of it also has to do with simply being outpaced by the world and not being able to differentiate oneself from the competition.

I have strong nostalgic feelings for small-town Arkansas diners. There aren't many more out there, but I understand, conceptually, why this is. If we're being honest, they're just heating up Sysco biscuits and warming a box of pre-made gravy. They slowly started losing the charm, kept the same prices in spite of inflation, went from homemade to food-service—and in the end McDonald's came in and offered the same thing for cheaper.

The good news is that there's a wave of small businesses out there that really do get it. There are people starting to build companies based around niche, high-end needs. Perhaps the small-town barber was driven out of business by a Sport Clips franchise, but down the street a kickass new hairstylist is charging men $30 for a haircut—his shop is booked solid for the next month. Perhaps the small-town bank was driven out of business by the new Bank of America branch, but a team of Russian nerds started a totally digital bank that lives in your pocket.

While it's alright to wax nostalgic about the missing things of yesteryear, let's make sure we're doing it in a sustainable manner. Everyone can do as they like with their own money (it's why we have it, after all) but when we're throwing our money at small businesses that don't do a better job—with better products and better service—those small businesses are just running on borrowed time.

The best solution is to create small businesses that provide unique value that cannot be paralleled by any conglomerate. That's the sort of business you want to start!

When you first decide to start your own company, you'll likely do a lot of searches and a lot of reading. Maybe you'll even search for something like "how to start a marketing agency." I know I did. Unfortunately, I got about 0% value from the countless hours I spent researching. The majority of agency success stories weren't applicable to us. It seemed like every successful new agency was created by someone splitting off from an already-established agency, taking a few clients with them.

We weren't coming from an agency. We had no existing business, only experience in the field, a few years of freelance marketing, and a burning desire to get out of the nine-to-five corporate world.

While the nine-to-five is a perfectly great option for many, it has never resonated with us. The reality is, unless you're working for an incredibly progressive company, your work will always make more for your boss than it makes for you. There's nothing wrong with that, if you can be upfront and honest about it. But if you want more (like earnings that aren't tied to showing up at work every day), then you've got to break out on your own. Or, at least, find a job working for a truly visionary leader who knows the value of risk and reward.

We didn't have a client to bring along into our roster. We had to do this by ourselves—this is the part that is almost never covered in articles on building agencies from scratch. We didn't have a clue how to do this. We were truly grasping for straws.

Here's how it ended up happening.

We cold called. We ran a few advertisement campaigns. We signed up for VIP accounts on marketing forums. We did a lot of content marketing (writing articles on our own site, social media activity, and researching search engine keywords to rank for). We signed up for online gig provider services.

Cold calling did absolutely nothing. It was a waste of time. Why? I think it's just an issue of statistics. The first level is finding someone who is actually needing your services (at this level, you could expect a hit rate of around 2-3%). The second level is finding someone who will pick you (if they need your services, you could expect around a 20% conversion rate into actually picking you). That means that to get a single customer, you'd need to cold call a total of 166 qualified businesses. We simply did not have the time for this. A single person could perhaps manage a hundred calls in a week, leaving no time for actually getting anything else done. That's what, three clients a month? With no guarantees they'll be spending enough to be worth your time.

That's not even considering the fact that I'm a terrible cold caller. I might be friendly, but I am also an introvert. Cold calls work for certain people and personalities. But we don't really want the sort of clients that cold calling typically gets: we'd prefer fewer clients at higher levels of service.

We also ran a handful of ad campaigns, both display and sponsored posts, on a couple niche websites. It was worth testing, because you never know if it works unless you try it—but in hindsight, it wasn't a great idea for a fledgling digital marketing company. Why advertise when your entire niche is advertising the same way, and they've got an ad budget of millions? Advertising for yourself will only work when you've got the budget and the branding behind a serious campaign—it's what we tell clients, after all!

We also bought premium memberships at a few niche sites and forums. This, surprisingly, wasn't a total waste of time. It did produce quite a few leads, projects, and clients, but they were so low-quality that after the first few months, it wasn't worth the hassle. We did this because we had to, and it's something I recommend in your beginning months; but in the end, we knew we were looking for larger fish.

We also did a lot of content marketing, writing dozens of articles on our own brand new site. And this was actually pretty surprising. Three months in, we started ranking on the second page of Google for some fairly valuable keywords. We did no SEO, no backlinks, just long-form original articles and case studies. It was a lot of work, and a lot of time spent writing and researching; but after a few months, we started seeing significant organic traffic. After a year, we ranked second (only to Bing Ads itself!) for the term "bing ads management."

We also started offering services at gig sites. This was a total surprise to us. The key to success here is to not depend upon the site for income by itself: that's not the point. The point is to upsell clients to become dedicated fans, and that's what we strove for. Within two months, we were making several thousand dollars just from these gig sites, and converting around 20% of these gigs into monthly contracts.

Lastly, we used our personal networking to gain clients and identify industry verticals we wanted to be a part of. Even if you don't have a whole lot of personal or professional connections, you might be surprised at just how many people actually do need your services, and already trust your ability to provide them. Starting a company is a big thing, and you'll be surprised how many people may help you along this path. The good thing about personal networking is that, although you're limited by volume, you'll find that these are the highest quality, highest-profile clients that you land.

The hard part about the whole thing was that it wasn't easy. It was a lot of work. It was even more time. Each of us spent 30-40 hours a week on building our site, our strategy, interacting with clients, building reports, campaigns, proposals, and accounting—on top of our full-time jobs. To be honest, for the first two months, I didn't think it was going to work. We were essentially working double time for no results. Week after week after week. I wanted to quit, several times. And then it just started happening.

We had promised ourselves that one of us would quit when we got a stable monthly average of $1,000 in income (huge goals, right?). For a couple months, it seemed like this would never happen. Then, suddenly, we were at double our goal. Anya put in her notice at her job. And before she was even finished there, we were at four times our goal. And, a couple months later, before I was able to put in my notice, we were already making far more than our previous full-time incomes combined. A year later, we were managing over a million dollars in annual ad spend, and it kept scaling up from there.

There are a few things that are important to remember when starting off. First, is that I'm not sure we could have done this if we were shackled by debt. Many Americans under the age of 30 have significant student loans, mortgages, or car loans: and if you need constant cash flow to keep your head above water, I couldn't really advise it. The stress was already insane: I can't imagine how I could have slept at night, knowing I had a student loan payment to make.

Second, liquid savings is essential. I learned this the hard way. I freelanced for almost five years right after graduation, and it was a slog at best. I didn't have much of a buffer for the slow months, and while I *was* able to tread water, I think I spent more time stressed than not being stressed.

Third, I don't think it's the best idea to do this right out of school. I tried going my own way once when I was 22, and finally when I was 27. In hindsight, I matured a lot in those five in-between years. I would have been better served by working the grind, networking on another company's dime, and seeing how the old dudes did it for a while. I have always been entrepreneurial, and always a bit of a terrible employee, but I should have bitten the bullet and just pulled a paycheck for a while. That's what Anya did, and she turned out just fine.

Fourth, don't go into debt and don't take out a loan for your business. I've seen others do it, and I've seen them bankrupted as a result. If your service business isn't good enough to sustain itself *without* a loan, it won't be good enough to sustain itself *with* a loan. Plus, service businesses simply have no operating costs to worry about, and high profit margins. You probably already have a laptop and a phone. All you need is time. Don't make your stress level worse by going into debt over your idea!

Fifth, don't worry about failure. I've started dozens of projects that have failed. Keep on trying!

REGISTERING YOUR COMPANY & BANK ACCOUNTS

There are a lot of unknowns about starting your own company. If you haven't done it before, the entire concept seems expensive, time consuming, complicated, and maybe a little risky. The good news? It's pretty easy.

A few simple steps are all that lie between where you are now and owning a company. If everyone knew how easy it was to set up the legal and financial part of a company, well, I think a lot of small business lawyers would be looking for work. The hard part comes after you set up the legal structure—the actual work!

The first thing you'll want to do is determine which sort of business structure you need. If you're just soloing, you actually aren't required to do anything—you can operate as a sole proprietor and pay taxes on self-employment income without any other paperwork or hassle. However, it's usually a good idea to incorporate an actual company. An LLC (limited liability company) will help you shield yourself from liabilities, enable you to purchase business equipment, set up business banking accounts, and look a little more professional while you do so.

It doesn't cost a lot. The annual registration cost depends upon your state, but we pay around $150 a year. The process? Go to your secretary of state's website, fill out a form, pay the fee. Then go to the IRS and request an Employer Identification Number (EIN) which you can use instead of a social security number for your tax forms.

Once you've got your company registered and an EIN (this usually takes a couple hours at most), you can open a business banking account. Head to your local bank and hand them the paperwork—I think it took me about 15 minutes before I had an account and a stack of temporary checks. Within a week, you have a business debit card and a real checkbook, and you're ready to go.

Of course, this is only part of the process—because you've got to get paid, as well. It's fairly simple to deposit a check, but in the digital world, these are fading away fast. You can either get paid by bank transfer (really only used in the United States for larger amounts), checks, credit card, or PayPal.

We find that PayPal is incredibly useful to have, since many clients prefer it. However, it's also more expensive (with rates around 4.5%) than other credit card processors (like Stripe, which is usually around 3%). At Discosloth, we use Wave for our credit card billing. The total cost is under 3% and has been extremely reliable.

Why bother with credit cards and these relatively high fees? When I freelanced, the ability to invoice via credit card wasn't really there yet. It was extremely difficult to set up a merchant account, and there weren't any services like Stripe that enabled you to easily set up an invoicing environment. So, I depended upon checks, PayPal, and bank transfers. My typical time between invoicing and collecting payment was between 2 and 4 weeks.

That's a difficult amount of time when you have to get a project done and you want to get paid. And it's even more difficult when people don't pay, and you have to chase them down, and it takes days or weeks before you even know if the payment went through. That's the benefit of credit card billing: at Discosloth, our average time from invoiced to paid is now 3 days. That's great for cash flow. Most of our clients are set up on automated billing, so it's an easy monthly process that runs itself—less hassle for them and for us. The downside is that we spend thousands and thousands a year on credit card fees, but I think the benefits outweigh the cost.

Building an agency—or any other form of marketing company —requires a huge leap of faith. However, the obvious risks come with obvious rewards, and for those who are daring enough to try it out and willing to put in the necessary hours in order to succeed—you might be surprised at your success!

THE FUTURE OF WORK

"Let us accept our own responsibility for the future." - John F. Kennedy

Work is changing. And, if you're just now getting into marketing, you're entering into a rapidly changing environment that will look totally different at the end of your career than it looked in the beginning.

Mid-range jobs—especially the sort of white-collar jobs that a marketer will be working in—are migrating away from traditional employment to freelance, self-employed, or small business roles.

As humans, people follow whichever path offers the most return with the least resistance: a balance of risk and reward. All of us do it on a fundamental level. Depending upon your fabric, you either tend towards risk (with potential high reward), or stability (but no unexpected rewards).

For an employer, your employees are making decisions based upon this fundamental rubric every day. For every benefit afforded by steady nine-to-five employment, there is also a trade-off. The benefits of being an employee (a stable income) are balanced out with some sacrifices (lower overall income, inflexibility, and lack of independence).

The most productive and innovative employees will eventually leave for either greater compensation at other companies, or the greater risk/reward of alternative income.

Although it's not an entirely perfect comparison, you can compare the employee-vs-employer relationship with a checking account-vs-investment account relationship. One is stable, but is losing money, usually not even seeing enough interest to make up for inflation. With a checking account, you'll never be surprised with a sudden windfall, just a steady trickle of interest. An investment account, on the other hand, has significant risk. But you'll see a much higher return over time along with the possibility of massive windfalls (and yes, possibly losing it all, too).

What's easily overlooked is that the risk-seeking type of employee—the one most likely to leave a company for greener pastures—is probably woven from the same fabric as the person who started your company in the first place. The employees most likely to create new products, start new departments, develop new initiatives, and show strong leadership are also the most likely to leave alltogther.

At some point, the benefits of independence begin to outweigh the benefits of traditional employment. And, globally, we're starting to see the emerging trend of workers shifting away from old-fashioned nine-to-five jobs and going into freelance, self-employment, small businesses, or startups.

In today's world, self-employment is in a bull market while traditional employment is entering a very bearish market. However, it's important to note that not all jobs are shifting. Entry-level jobs will continue to be filled by freshly-graduated employees (in my opinion, these are the entry-level positions that are task-oriented rather than relationship-, management-, or strategy-oriented). The same goes with very high-level jobs, and this is why senior employees will continue to be employed at large companies (this is the elite level of programmers, VPs, and relationship-based executives).

But what about the middle—the rest of them, employees with mid-level experience, but high ambition? I see a strong shift towards independence rather than stability, at least for mid-career professionals, and it might be interesting to pull apart the threads and ask why this shift is taking place.

I think the most obvious answer is a financial one: it's becoming much easier to make more money on your own rather than working for someone else.

We're seeing an exponential increase in decentralization. For better or worse, the old way of cubicles, time cards, and thirty-year single-company careers is dying out. Workers are learning that, perhaps, their money doesn't have to be tied to their time.

It's important to analyze some of the events that shaped the upbringing of today's young professional. I remember many of my college peers telling me in 2008 that the college funds nurtured by their parents for years had just been wiped out. A handful of other peers had parents with underwater mortgages, repossessed cars, or retirement savings eliminated.

I suspect that this is a huge reason why many younger workers don't really care about locking their money into 401(k)s, putting too much into low-return mutual funds, or trapping themselves with a stifling mortgage. We saw a generation of workers slaving 50 hours a week in corporate America, only to lose it all back to the beast.

One good thing is that offshoring is no longer something only the absurdly wealthy can do: anyone can move to countries with higher income potential and continue the work they did before. As a marketer, you can take advantage of this too!

Those who've left the nine-to-five don't want to work 50 hours a week for the beast: they would rather work for themselves, and decide whether to work 30 hours or 80 hours per week. But this independence is part of the reward for the risk: increased flexibility, higher income, greater independence, and the astonishing ability to build anything, anywhere, thanks to a burgeoning decentralization of communication.

I haven't worked in an office since 2011. I've worked from a lot of tables—in coffeeshops, cafes, living rooms, and hotel rooms. But no office. As freelancers, employees, and as business owners, we simply haven't needed a traditional office! Just about everywhere in the world has internet fast enough to let you communicate with your coworkers and clients, and that's exactly what I've done for the past decade.

This saves money for everyone—as an employee, your boss is having to spend precious revenue in order to maintain that expensive office lease, and that's money that doesn't go to your pockets. As an employer, every dime you spend is a dime that isn't profit. Spending even a modest $1000 a month on an office adds up.

When economic recessions roll around, as they inevitably do, marketing agencies are among the first to go. Reducing overhead is a crucial way of preventing that from happening to you.

Not all work will end up remote; the vast majority of jobs actually won't. There are many reasons for this: sometimes people like going to an office, sometimes jobs are location-dependent, sometimes working remotely doesn't mesh with company cultures or individual cultures, or sometimes it's just not very efficient. But many jobs will. If a job mostly consists of sitting in front of a computer, or talking on the phone, there's little reason it can't be done from home.

I suspect marketing is done best when it's executed in a creative, free-form environment rather than inside a cubicle. Even if you choose to work in a traditional setting, most of your freelancers, colleagues, and competitors aren't going to be. So it's important to be able to adjust to their work status—realistic expectations will help workflow, camaraderie, and overall efficiency.

Regardless of the specifics, the most important thing to remember is that everything changes, and industries on the cusp of technology change even faster. What is changing today will be the norm of tomorrow—and old news in a couple of years.

AFTERWORD

Marketing is not perfect. It's actually quite flawed. But it's got incredible potential, and it has the benefit of being one of those industries in which a little cleverness and intuition go a long way.

Breaking into marketing is always difficult. At some point, everyone is a brand-new beginner. Even halfway through your career, everything will change and you'll have to relearn concepts or strategies. But in the end, if you keep at it, it will pay off.

We love marketing—how unique you can be, how tech-focused you can be, how data-centric you can be, and perhaps most of all, how many opportunities you can find. We encourage everyone who wants to become a digital marketer to keep their eyes wide open and grab hold of those opportunities when they appear!

Gil & Anya
Lake Como, Italy
March 2019

gil@discosloth.com
anya@discosloth.com

PART III:
APPENDIX

MARKETING RESOURCES

Over the years, we've collected a large index of resources for digital marketers. Some of these are simply good blogs to follow, and others are very specific guides for a particular digital marketing discipline. We're well aware that this book is printed, so you can't exactly click on the links. We're very sorry, indeed.

MARKETING BLOGS

SparkToro
www.sparktoro.com
Rand Fishkin, original writer of the Beginner's Guide To SEO and founder of Moz, next cofounded SparkToro as a tool to provide more info and data for the influencer marketing industry. He also blogs regularly. It's worth keeping up on his insights on SEO.

Thunderhead Works
www.thunderheadworks.com
Tom Peterson, interviewed in this book, writes solid content on general marketing theory and communication. It's not digitally focused, but his years of experience as a marketing director provides

some crucial insight into theory that anyone in marketing will find useful.

Moz Blog
www.moz.com/blog
One of the most valuable online resources for white-hat search engine optimization, with guest posts from a variety of well-respected marketers.

Kellogg Insight
https://insight.kellogg.northwestern.edu
For a high-level look at marketing theory, this is one of the best resources we've found. It's not very actionable or practical, to be honest, but that's to be expected from an academic site. It's still interesting and insightful, though.

MARKETING BOOKS

Blink - Malcolm Gladwell

Today's world is filled with a lot of data; sometimes, it can be too much data. Even though digital marketers have a massively valuable ability to sort through endless amounts of data, being too close to it can result in poor decisions, and that's exactly what this book is about. Expertise goes a long way in making decisions, and spreadsheets don't always tell the whole story. An excellent resource to help prevent yourself from becoming too myopic.

Lost and Founder - Rand Fishkin

We've read a lot of books by influential thinkers in the tech and marketing worlds. Many founders go either one of two ways when they're writing memoirs or reflections on their industry: they're either blatantly self-aggrandizing ("look at my sick Learjet!") or they're buried in technicalities and politics and unable to see the big picture. Either way, self-awareness is a rare quality. This book is very self-aware: sometimes painfully so. It's honest, transparent, and uncomfortable. It's worth it alone to hear an insider's opinion on the realities of venture capital vs bootstrapping.

Zero To One - Peter Thiel
A book developed from class notes from a course Peter Thiel, cofounder of PayPal, taught at Stanford, this short volume expounds on the simple concept of zero to one (creation) being more fundamentally productive than anything beyond that. It's a critical look at how simply creating things is a net benefit. I found it very insightful from a business perspective.

Trust Me, I'm Lying - Ryan Holiday
A guerrilla marketing expert and former American Apparel marketer, the often-controversial takes by Ryan Holiday are still extremely important. From a purely psychological basis, understanding how marketing and PR influences the public conversation can help you in everything from content creation to ad writing.

On Writing - Stephen King
That's right, it's not about marketing and it's not by a marketer. But this is one of the best books out there on clear communication, succinct writing, and how to get things done.

Marketing Guides

The Beginner's Guide To PPC

www.discosloth.com/beginners-guide-to-ppc

Our very own guide, which we crafted with loving care and hope that everyone thinks it's as good as we do. It's our baby, but it's also been called "the sort of content I wish I'd created" and "If you need a resource for those learning PPC, this is the one." That obviously means you need to read it, too.

Beginner's Guide To SEO

www.moz.com/beginners-guide-to-seo

The original guide itself, rewritten over the years to keep up with the times, is still one of the most valuable resources out there. It was the inspiration behind our PPC guide, and Anya even had it printed out for reference when she was first diving into digital marketing.

Google Best Practices

support.google.com/adwords

Google's closest answer to a guide. This will provide helpful information if you're looking for specific insight into how to use AdWords.

Academy For Ads

https://academy.exceedlms.com

Google's new home for certifications and study guides. It's worth going through their Fundamentals course and a few others, and getting certified.

100+ Google Ranking Factors

www.zyppy.com/seo-success-factors

An SEO-focused resource on ranking factors. A very useful and very informed guide— it's worth learning about this, regardless of your specific niche!

MARKETING TOOLS

Answer The Public

www.answerthepublic.com

Answer The Public is a great keyword exploration tool which helps find similar terms, phrases, and semantic possibilities for your keywords.

SERPsim

www.serpsim.com

Our favorite online tool for visualizing how meta descriptions and titles look in Google's search results.

SparkToro Trending

www.sparktoro.com/trending

Not as much a tool as an incredible way to keep up with marketing news, Trending analyzes which links the most popular marketers are sharing on Twitter, and lists them daily.

CoSchedule Headline Analyzer

www.coschedule.com/headline-analyzer

A great tool for analyzing your email subject lines, giving insight about which words to use, and the appropriate link for maximum open rates.

Nibbler Website Test
nibbler.silktide.com
A useful tool to analyze your website, giving you a rundown of things like speed, page content, broken links, and a huge range of other tips for optimization. It's not a perfect tool, and some of the suggestions need to be ignored, but it's a good way to get a quick handle on a website's health.

Planable
www.planable.io
A collaboration tool for marketing teams to organize and schedule content for multiple social media channels.

MailChimp
www.mailchimp.com
The standard for email campaigns. It starts with a free plan, for up to 2000 subscribers, so it won't cost you anything for a long time.

REFERENCES

1 Thiel, Peter. "Zero To One: Notes on Startups, or How to Build the Future."

2 Surprisingly, languages like Mandarin or Hindi are absent from this list. That's because there's a lot of Mandarin or Hindi speakers on the internet, but not necessarily a lot of websites written in those languages.

3 Fishkin, Rand. "Why SEO Is Important—The Beginners Guide To SEO." https://moz.com/beginners-guide-to-seo/why-search-engine-marketing-is-necessary.

4 Dudharejia, Manish. "5 Things You Can Do Right Now to Improve Your Google E-A-T Rating." https://www.searchenginejournal.com/improve-google-eat-score/270711/

5 Gildner, Gil and Anya. "The Beginner's Guide To PPC." https://www.discosloth.com/beginners-guide-to-ppc/

6 Gildner, Anya. "Case Study: Increasing Organic Traffic by 22% YoY". https://www.discosloth.com/case-studies/increase-organic-leads-yoy.html

7 Gladwell, Malcolm. "Blink: The Power of Thinking Without Thinking." Back Bay Books, 2005.

8 Bradstreet, Kyle. "eps2.2_init_1.asec" Mr. Robot: Season 2, Episode 4. July 27, 2016.

[9] Godin, Seth. "The Dip: A Little Book That Teaches You When to Quit (and When to Stick)." Portfolio, 2007.

[10] Bradbury, Ray. "Fahrenheit 451." Quote from Juan Ramón Jiménez. Ballantine, 1953.

Made in the USA
Las Vegas, NV
07 September 2022

54882038R00121